P9-DCW-674

UNDER SIEGE!

Also by Andrea Warren

Escape from Saigon:
How a Vietnam War Orphan Became an American Boy

Orphan Train Rider: One Boy's True Story

Pioneer Girl: Growing Up on the Prairie

Surviving Hitler: A Boy in the Nazi Death Camps

We Rode the Orphan Trains

UNDER SIEGE!

THREE CHILDREN AT THE
CIVIL WAR BATTLE FOR VICKSBURG

BY ANDREA WARREN

WALLINGFORD PUBLIC LIBRARY
200 North Main St.
Wallingford, CT 06492

MELANIE KROUPA BOOKS
FARRAR STRAUS GIROUX
NEW YORK

CHILDREN'S LIBRARY

J973.734
WAR

A Note to Readers

In writing this book I have made every attempt to verify information. My sources include what people wrote about themselves and their experiences, and what others who knew them wrote of them. I also interviewed several experts on the Vicksburg campaign and studied the works of Civil War historians.

Copyright © 2009 by Andrea Warren
All rights reserved
Distributed in Canada by Douglas & McIntyre Ltd.
Printed in the United States of America
Designed by Robbin Gourley
First edition, 2009
10   9   8   7   6   5   4   3   2   1

www.fsgkidsbooks.com

Library of Congress Cataloging-in-Publication Data
Warren, Andrea.
    Under siege! : three children at the Civil War battle for Vicksburg / by Andrea Warren.— 1st ed.
        p.   cm.
    Includes bibliographical references and index.
    ISBN-13: 978-0-374-31255-8
    ISBN-10: 0-374-31255-9
    1. Vicksburg (Miss.)—History—Siege, 1863—Juvenile literature.   2. United States—History—Civil War, 1861–1865—Children—Juvenile literature.   3. Children—Mississippi—Vicksburg—History—19th century—Juvenile literature.   I. Title.

E475.27.W37 2009
973.7'344—dc22

                                                                                                2008001136

For Jay,
in loving memory

"Vicksburg is the key. The war can never be brought

to a close until that key is in our pocket.

We can take all the northern ports of the Confederacy, and they can

defy us from Vicksburg."

–President Abraham Lincoln

CONTENTS

UNDER SIEGE!

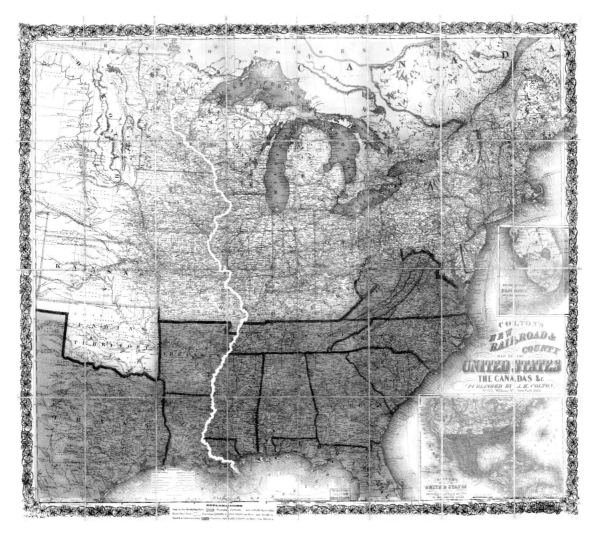

This map of the Confederate States, created in 1862, shows how the Mississippi River (shown in white) ran through the center of the Confederacy (the states outlined in dark gray), providing a great water highway. Once the North had seized New Orleans in April 1862 and Memphis two months later, only the guns at Vicksburg kept it from controlling the river. Silencing those guns was key to a Northern victory.

INTRODUCTION

T he first time I read about Vicksburg's role in the Civil War, I was amazed to learn that this American city had been under siege for forty-seven days. What happened at Vicksburg was not only important to the outcome of the war—it was also a great human story, for inside that besieged city were 5,000 townspeople, including an estimated 1,000 children.

I am interested in the Civil War, in part because my great-grandfather, John Wesley Forest, fought in it. He was a Yankee from Vermont, and thankfully he was not injured. Though he could not have known it at the time, the war he participated in would be *the* pivotal event in the history of America, determining whether we would become one country or two. Amazingly, perhaps miraculously, we managed to emerge as one.

But the price paid by both sides was appalling, and it wasn't just soldiers like my great-grandfather who paid it. Civilians often sacrificed as much or more. Families lost their soldier fathers, uncles, and brothers who died from injury and disease. In the South, where much of the war was fought, countless people lost their homes and businesses and were plunged into poverty. Wherever there was fighting, civilians were in danger, and many died. In the forty-seven-day siege of Vicksburg, everyone, including the children, endured tremendous hardships. To escape the shells raining down on them day and night, many lived in caves. Starvation threatened to kill them if the explosions did not.

I have always had a special interest in the stories of children in war because my adopted daughter was orphaned by the Vietnam War. In tribute to her and to all children caught up in the chaos of war, I wanted to tell the story of Vicksburg, as much as possible, through the eyes of children who were there. You will meet three of them: Lucy McRae, the ten-year-old daughter of a well-to-do Vicksburg merchant; Willie Lord, the eleven-year-old son of an Episcopal minister; and Frederick Grant, the twelve-year-old son of the Union general, Ulysses S. Grant, who was with his father during much of the Vicksburg campaign. Lucy and Willie endured hunger, fear, desperation, and brushes with death. Fred saw the horrors of war firsthand, suffering from illness and a bullet wound.

All three wrote or spoke about their experiences. Lucy said, "Although I was only a little girl, many striking incidents were indelibly impressed upon my mind. I have often had the question asked me, 'How do you remember so much about the siege?' My answer is that, being shut up in the place, living in a cave under the ground for six weeks . . . I do not think a child could have passed through what I did and have forgotten it."

I wish all three children had told us more about themselves, or that I could travel back in time to talk to them, for I have many unanswered questions. I have supplemented their testimony with information from others who were present during the campaign for Vicksburg—townspeople, and soldiers and generals from both sides. I went to Vicksburg and interviewed local experts about what life was like for children back then. I walked where Lucy, Willie, Fred, and all the others in this story walked. I explored the military park and experienced the intense Mississippi summer weather and wondered how they did it—how the Northerners, in their heavy wool uniforms, endured the sweltering heat and humidity of the swamps and bogs, and how the Southerners, terrorized by the shelling and with food supplies dwindling, survived at all.

You are about to be transported back to 1862 and 1863, to a little city on the banks of the Mississippi River. What happened there, what the armies of the North and South, the townspeople and children, experienced there, helped determine the course of the war and the shape of what we have become today: an imperfect, often racist, freedom-loving nation, but with one government, one constitution, and one flag—the *United* States of America.

As shown in this 1862 drawing, Vicksburg was a prosperous little city on the banks of the Mississippi River (far right).

WAR COMES TO VICKSBURG

December 1862

From the top of Sky Parlor Hill, ten-year-old Lucy McRae closed one eye and peered through her spyglass at the Mississippi River. She looked as far as she could see in both directions.

Was the enemy out there somewhere? Would *this* be the day that Yankee gunboats steamed into view to attack her town?

But she saw only the usual river traffic—barges, flatboats, a sailing ship or two. Had the Yankees realized they could never silence the guns at Vicksburg?

No one believed that. Sooner or later, everyone said, the enemy would be back.

Though Lucy could view the river from the second-floor porch of her home in Vicksburg, Mississippi, on a clear day she could see for fifty miles from the top of Sky Parlor Hill. This was the favored spot of well-to-do residents who lived in nearby homes high in the hills of this very hilly river town, and some of Lucy's neighbors were usually there. Everyone was watchful these days. When the weather was warm, the climb up the steep wooden steps to the top of the hill was punishing for ladies wearing tight corsets and high-button shoes, and carrying silk parasols to keep the strong

Lucy McRae.

sun from darkening their delicate skin. But they still came. On winter days like today, with a cold early December wind blowing off the river, they wore capes and gloves. Even with a hat over her blond curls, Lucy could hear the rustling of their silk skirts atop layers of petticoats.

Since she attended the all-girls academy in town, it was usually later in the day before she could get to the hill. Sometimes her brothers Colin, who was fourteen, and Fulton, twelve, were there when she arrived. Both boys were excited about the war and planned to join the Confederate army just as soon as their parents allowed it. Lucy's two oldest brothers, Allen and John, both in their early twenties, were already in the army. Fortunately, John was stationed right here at Vicksburg. But Allen's regiment was far away in Virginia. The family worried all the time about him. One of these days they might have to worry about John as well.

Many in Vicksburg had mixed feelings about the war—some were even pro-Union—but out of loyalty to their families and community they supported the Confederacy. Mississippi had been the second state to secede. When the war had started in the summer of 1861, nobody had thought it would last more than a month or two. Southerners agreed that the North needed to be taught a lesson, and the South would do it swiftly and surely. Gradually, however, it became clear that this would be a long struggle, and that much of it would be fought on Southern soil. Now, in December 1862, Yankee bluecoats were steadily moving into Mississippi from the north. Their stated objective was to capture Vicksburg and silence the cannon guarding the Mississippi River, keeping it from Union control. Lucy knew that her little city was of such strategic importance that sooner or later the Yankees would attack.

✳ ✳ ✳

EARLY LAST APRIL, townspeople had seen firsthand the awful consequences of war. Rebel troops had bravely fought the Yankees at the bloody two-day battle of Shiloh in southwestern Tennessee, but had been defeated by the Union generals Ulysses Grant and William T. Sherman. The next day, trains rolled into Vicksburg, their cars spilling over with badly wounded Rebel soldiers. Townspeople helped the Catholic Sisters of Mercy care for the survivors at Vicksburg's two hospitals and also helped bury the dead. Families like Lucy's, confronted with the realities of the battlefield, now worried even more about their own boys. Lucy had not been allowed to see the wounded soldiers, but she had heard townspeople talking about how young they were—some even younger than her brothers—and she saw the fear in her parents' eyes.

Before the war, life in Vicksburg had been quite pleasant for the McRae family. For anyone traveling on the Mississippi River, a first glimpse of this city was always an impressive sight. The town's hills and bluffs rose 200 feet in the air. The majestic courthouse and even some of the elegant homes high in the hills were visible from the water. With 5,000 residents, Vicksburg was the second largest city in Mississippi. Lucy described it as "a place of education, culture, and luxury." There were several opulent hotels, an opera house, fine grocery stores, six newspapers, and several private educational academies. The new courthouse, built by slave labor, had been completed just two years earlier, and its impressive dome, said to be the height of St. Paul's Cathedral in London, dominated the skyline.

Though the North had imposed a blockade on Southern ports after the start of the war, preventing the arrival of foreign merchandise, townspeople still had their choice of banks, pharmacies, tailors, shoe stores, liquor stores, and gunsmith shops. Dressmakers and the millinery shop were open for business. The candy store still had treats, and the bookstore was still stocked with books—just not the latest offerings from publishers in New York or London.

*Travelers along
the river were
always impressed
by their first
glimpse of
Vicksburg and
the magnificent
courthouse high
in its hills.*

Lucy's father was a prosperous businessman. Lucy was the youngest of William and Indiana McRae's five children and the only girl. She admitted that she was spoiled. When she went downtown with her mother to shop, the contrast between her life and the lives of poor children in the city was apparent. As Rice, the family's house slave, carefully eased their horse-drawn carriage down the steep streets, Lucy saw the dilapidated homes of children too poor to go to school. Most of them could not read or write and had to work at whatever menial jobs they could find, earning only pennies a day. Near the river, Lucy saw seedy hotels and cotton warehouses. Sailors and dockworkers milled about, and the air smelled of coal smoke and tar.

Before the war, steamboats landed at the docks several times a day, releasing a colorful stew of passengers—gamblers, businessmen, and families traveling the river between Memphis, 200 miles to the north, and New

Orleans, 200 miles to the south. Now the Yankees controlled those two ports, and, though there was still river traffic, there were no more steamboats going back and forth to those cities.

Since the start of the war, Lucy had gotten used to the sight of the cannon that stood guard on the bluffs and on the waterfront to protect the river from the Yankees. And anywhere she went, she saw soldiers. More were arriving all the time. There were now 10,000 Confederate troops stationed around the perimeter of Vicksburg to safeguard the city and its guns. The Mississippi River was vital to the Southern cause. It started in Minnesota and flowed 2,000 miles to the Gulf of Mexico, and the North now controlled all of it but this small section at Vicksburg. If Federal troops could seize control of Vicksburg, they could split the South down the mid-

Before the blockade, Vicksburg was a busy riverport. During the blockade, the cost of basic staples like sugar, salt, and coffee soared.

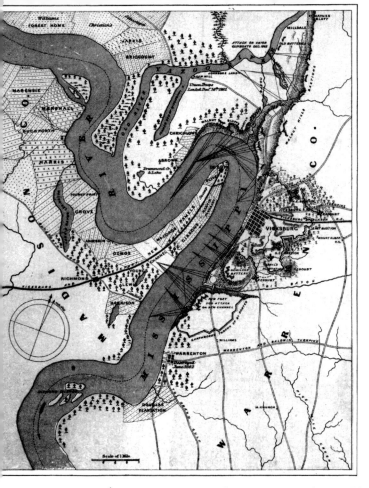

This 1863 map shows Vicksburg's location on the Mississippi River, the hairpin curve just north of the city, and the location of the Confederate batteries along the bluffs and shoreline.

dle, into an eastern half and a western half. The Mississippi River would become their highway, giving them a direct route to invade the Deep South.

When planning strategy with his generals, President Abraham Lincoln had said, "Vicksburg is the key. The war can never be brought to a close until that key is in our pocket. We can take all the northern ports of the Confederacy, and they can defy us from Vicksburg." It was only a question of how and when the North's all-out assault would occur.

Vicksburg intended to be ready. Because of its location, reaching it would be a challenge for the enemy, for it was surrounded by swamps, ravines, and steep gullies. The river was the more obvious path of invasion, but it flooded in hard rains and its currents were treacherous to navigate. If enemy boats came from the north, they had to slow down just before reaching Vicksburg to negotiate a hairpin curve in the river. This made them easier targets for the huge cannon on the bluffs and the smaller cannon along the waterfront—a total of forty big guns in all.

Still, the Yankees had tried, and would try again.

✳ ✳ ✳

NO ONE IN VICKSBURG would forget their first attempt. One day the previous May, several gunboats had steamed into view and dropped anchor. A delegation of Union officers climbed into a small boat. Waving a white flag so no one would open fire on them, they handed over a demand that the city surrender. From Vicksburg had come the reply, "Mississippians don't know and refuse to learn how to surrender. If the

Federal commanders think they can teach [us] otherwise, let them come and try."

The Union officers had been surprised, thinking that once they had their boats in position opposite the town, surrender would quickly follow. But the Confederates knew the Union guns were not powerful enough to damage the Vicksburg cannon. And just as suspected, the gunboats lobbed a few harmless shells at the town and then gave up and went away.

While townspeople had breathed a sigh of relief, they knew the boats were a warning of what was to come. In preparation, additional Confederate troops arrived to shore up protection of the guns and the city, and more cannon were added to strengthen the artillery batteries on the bluffs and along the waterfront. Some folks boarded up their homes and moved to the country. Most stayed—out of defiance, to protect their property, or because they had nowhere else to go.

If the Union intended to bombard the city, then townspeople had to find protection. They realized that caves would be the safest place. The Vicksburg soil was soft and easy to dig in, and some people already had caves that they used for storage. The idea of taking shelter in the ground wasn't appealing—caves were hot, dirty, and full of bugs and snakes. But that was better than being exposed to exploding shells.

After that first Yankee assault, cave digging began in earnest. People wanted their caves to be as close to their homes as possible so they could get to them quickly. There were so many hills in Vicksburg that it was not hard to find a location. Slaves dug many of the caves that now began to dot the landscape. Most were ordered to do so by their owners, but a few were paid for this task and allowed to keep the money. Joe Davis, the brother of Confederate president Jefferson Davis, owned a plantation near Vicksburg. When there was still steamboat traffic on the river, he had allowed his slaves to sell wood, eggs, and produce from their gardens to the passengers and to keep their meager earnings. But most slaves allowed to work for money earned only enough to make their lives a little easier by purchasing needed food and clothing, for the average slave was both undernourished

and poorly dressed. Still, there were rare stories of slaves saving enough money to purchase their own freedom. About fifty freed blacks lived in Vicksburg. Almost all of them had been given freedom by their former masters, and they lived simply, usually doing odd jobs to support themselves. Several had special skills as bricklayers or blacksmiths.

Apart from these few exceptions, slavery was a fact of life in the agricultural South, and children like Lucy who grew up with slavery usually did not question it. Most slaves lived on plantations and worked in the fields. Those lucky enough to be house servants enjoyed a higher status. They worked as cooks, maids, butlers, and drivers, and as mammies

This photograph, taken in 1862, shows five generations of one Southern black family.

who cared for their white owners' children. Lucy's family owned Rice and also owned a slave named Mary Ann. Rice and Mary Ann had separate shacks behind the McRae home that were nicer than most slave cabins on plantations, and they had better food and clothing. But they were still slaves, and as their owners, Lucy's parents could punish them or sell them if they wished.

Lucy knew how much Rice, especially, wanted his freedom. For him, the arrival of the Yankees could signal a whole new life.

✳ ✳ ✳

IN JUNE 1862, six weeks after their first attack, the Yankees returned. This time they came not only with more boats but also with more powerful guns. As the fleet steamed into view, hundreds of people hurried to Sky Parlor Hill. They watched in shock and horror as the iron-clads opened fire.

Lucy's mother had wanted to leave Vicksburg when the gunboats had appeared the first time, but Mr. McRae had firmly refused. When the gunboats came back in June, Lucy was at home when she heard the first explosion. As an adult she recalled, "One bright afternoon men, women and children could be seen seeking the hilltops with spyglasses, as from the heights could be seen a black object slowly approaching along the river. Suddenly a shell came rattling over as if to say, 'Here I am!'

"My mother was much alarmed, but still faithful to womanly curiosity, stood on the upper porch of our house to see the gunboat, if possible. Another shell, and still another, and the hills began to be deserted.

"The gunboat, seeing that her shells were falling short, ventured a little closer, and sent a few shells into the town. People sought their homes, but sleep visited few, as the shelling continued until late that night.

"The next morning the shelling began very early, and the women and children were to be seen running by every road that led out of the town."

Lucy and her family stayed put. For two long days the Union fleet hurled shells at Vicksburg. Loud, thunderous booms, one after another, rattled windows and numbed eardrums. Shells knocked holes through the walls of houses, damaged the Methodist church, tore up sidewalks, and blasted craters in yards. Lucy's home was not damaged, but she grieved with townspeople over the death of a woman well known in the community who was killed by a shell as she ran for safety.

Finally, guns blazing, the Federal ships managed to fight their way past the Vicksburg batteries, but their crews suffered casualties, and what had been gained? Any ships that tried to do the same would face the same. The Federal commander felt Vicksburg could only be taken by attack from both land and river. As for the bombardment of the city, he felt it had served no purpose. The guns of Vicksburg were still in place.

That had been six months ago. Now it was December, and as Lucy looked through her spyglass from Sky Parlor Hill, her warm coat buttoned to her chin, all was quiet below her. The Confederacy still controlled the river.

These sailors onboard the USS Mendota, *a steam-driven gunboat, saw action in the battle for Richmond. While fewer sailors than soldiers lost their lives in the war, naval service was demanding and full of peril. Most naval battles were fought within sight of land— either along the coast, in bays, or in Southern rivers like the Mississippi.*

Eggnog parties were popular in the South during the Christmas season.

THE CHRISTMAS EVE BALL

December 24, 1862

Vicksburg dressed up for Christmas. The Yankees might not be far away, but this beloved holiday would go on as always. Garlands, wreaths, and holly decorated the classic black iron grillwork and stately white columns of the town's most prominent homes. Just as they had for generations, families planned to celebrate the holiday by attending special church services, hosting eggnog parties, singing Christmas carols, decorating Christmas trees, and lighting the Yule log. Holiday dinners would include turkey, ham, oysters, plenty of side dishes, and gingerbread, custard pies, sponge cake, and plum pudding. Vicksburg gentlemen would still have their fine Southern cigars and Southern bourbon to finish off a splendid meal.

Because of the blockade, society women could not order new gowns from Paris to wear to the annual Christmas Eve Ball, but in spite of this, everyone was in a festive mood. The Yankees didn't seem like much of a threat at the moment. Their leader, General Ulysses Grant, who had defeated the Confederates at Shiloh, had set up a huge supply base at Holly Springs, Mississippi, near the Tennessee border, and no doubt thought he could attack Vicksburg from there. But in a daring raid just days earlier, the Rebels had destroyed the base, forcing Grant to retreat to Memphis.

The ball was a wonderful way to celebrate this victory, and on Christmas Eve, the elite of the city bundled up against the cold and blustery weather and climbed into their carriages. They made their way along the steep streets to the stately mansion of Dr. and Mrs. William Balfour, where they were greeted by their hosts. The mansion's ballroom was festooned with fragrant, fresh-cut greenery. The lavish refreshment table, lighted by massive candelabra, groaned under the weight of meats, cakes, pies, and other sweets. Guests were served punch from Mrs. Balfour's elaborate silver punch bowl, and they sipped champagne and wine poured from exquisite cut-glass decanters.

Amid hoop skirts and dashing military uniforms, as the orchestra played merrily, guests were swept up in music, laughter, and dancing. At least for this one evening, they could quite easily believe that there was no war.

✯ ✯ ✯

SOMEWHERE UPRIVER, 30,000 Union soldiers in regulation blue were packed onto eighty ships. Those on deck huddled together miserably, pelted by cold rain, as the ships navigated through the rough black waters of the Mississippi River. Any holiday celebration for these bluecoats existed only in their memories of home and family. On this Christmas Eve, they were part of an army with a mission: they were going to take Vicksburg.

Their leader, General William Sherman, was following a plan he had hatched with General Grant. The Confederate commander of Vicksburg, General John Pemberton, had hurried his troops to northern Mississippi to pursue Grant. The plan was that while Grant engaged Pemberton, Sherman would take his troops downriver and quickly conquer Vicksburg, for without Pemberton and his army, the city had little defense.

But after beginning their river journey to Vicksburg, Sherman had no way of knowing that the Rebels had destroyed the Union's supply base at Holly Springs, as the telegraph wires had been cut. Grant had had to

retreat to Memphis instead of fighting Pemberton. And now, Pemberton was on his way back to Vicksburg.

On Christmas Eve, as dancers twirled merrily in the Balfours' ballroom, Sherman's flotilla was suddenly spotted by Confederates monitoring the river. They quickly sent a message through a private telegraph line to Phillip Hall, the telegraph operator on the Louisiana side of the Mississippi River, directly across from Vicksburg. It read, "Great God, Phil, eighty-one gunboats and transports have passed here tonight."

Hall knew what he had to do. Even though it was a stormy night and the river was dangerous, he risked his life to row a tiny boat to the Vicksburg wharf. Soaked to the skin and out of breath, he ran past the saloons and sagging hotels along the waterfront, past the downtown shops and stores, and then up the hilly streets to where Vicksburg's most privileged lived.

The ironclads— ships covered with protective metal—were a new innovation at the time of the Civil War.

Almost ready to collapse when he finally arrived at the Balfour home just after midnight, he ignored the surprised protests of the house slaves and burst into the ballroom. As he pushed his way through the happy throng of dancers, the music stopped and startled guests stared at the dripping wet man who was asking to speak to the officer in charge. Brigadier General Martin Luther Smith, second in command to Pemberton, stepped forward to confer with him. Then Smith's face grew pale. He shouted to the crowd, "The party is at an end. The enemy is coming down the river!"

Amid the shrieks and cries of the guests, Smith advised people to flee the city. Every soldier of every rank was immediately put on alert and told to report for duty. The ball was over. It might be Christmas, but Vicksburg was at war.

✹ ✹ ✹

GENERAL PEMBERTON was halfway back to Vicksburg when he learned that Sherman was also headed there. To be sure he arrived before the enemy, Pemberton raced his troops back to defend the city. He was just in time. Sherman's army had moved more slowly than anticipated and on Christmas Eve was still twenty miles north of Vicksburg. Over the next several days, the Union general eased his 30,000 men southward by boat, hoping to hear from Grant and trying to figure out a good place to put his troops ashore. Instead of solid land, he found mostly bogs and swamps. Finally he selected Chickasaw Bayou, three miles north of Vicksburg, where the land looked fairly stable. He still had not heard from Grant, and now he knew that Pemberton and his troops were back, for as soon as the Union bluecoats landed, soldiers in gray started lining up opposite them on the bayou's waterlogged ground.

When the fighting started on the morning of December 28, Sherman quickly saw that even though he had twice as many men as Pemberton, the Rebels had the advantage. They knew how to fight in swampy terrain. When Union troops tried to move forward, they lost their footing, sinking

into the marsh. Unused to such dense vegetation, they could not see what was ahead of them or around them. The spooky sounds of swamp birds and animals they didn't recognize kept them on edge. Trees were everywhere, growing right through the water and making it nearly impossible for the men to load and aim their guns. As a result, much of the fighting was brutal hand-to-hand combat.

Union troops depicted here struggled to get through unfamiliar swamps near Vicksburg.

To their surprise, Union soldiers discovered that a sharpshooter giving them trouble was a black man. A reporter for the *New York Herald* who was with the Union troops wrote: "He mounts a breastwork regardless of all danger, and getting sight of a Federal soldier, draws up his musket at arm's length and fires, never failing of hitting his mark . . . It is certain that Negroes are fighting here, though probably only as sharpshooters." This was unsettling to Northerners who assumed that all blacks supported the Union.

At the end of the first day, the Yankees had suffered almost 2,000 casualties, while the Rebels had lost only 187 men. That night both sides waited out the darkness. Fearful of revealing their positions, neither could light fires. The fog was thick. A cold, hard rain fell, and Yankees and Rebels alike suffered. Sherman assessed the situation. The river was rising and, with the threat of flooding, he knew his troops were in danger of drowning. If he tried another assault on Rebel lines, his men were sure to take heavy losses. With regret, he ordered his troops to withdraw.

He did not try to excuse what happened, writing later of his defeat at Chickasaw Bayou, "I reached Vicksburg at the time appointed, landed, assaulted, and failed." He said that the city was "the strongest place I ever saw . . . No place on earth is favored by nature with natural defenses as is Vicksburg."

The city's newspapers gave ecstatic accounts of the Rebel victory. Lucy joined the hoopla and celebration. The Rebs had won! They had *won*! Surely now the Yankees would go home.

Instead, townspeople soon realized that the Union army planned to spend the winter in Mississippi. Everyone knew that eventually they would try another assault.

It was more important than ever to keep an eye on the river. On Sky Parlor Hill, bundled against the cold, Lucy did her part.

THE GENERAL'S BOY GOES TO WAR

Spring 1863

At age twelve, Frederick Grant knew that he was lucky. Most military children rarely saw their fathers in wartime, but Ulysses Grant was a devoted family man and he wanted his wife and four children with him as often as possible—even if that brought them directly into the theater of war.

Some wives wanted nothing to do with the inferior housing and food that were part of military life—especially during a war—but Julia Grant didn't mind. "Whenever she could, Mother got as near to Father as possible," Fred recalled as an adult, noting that she willingly endured camp life and that she felt the experience was good for her children. During the summer of 1861, when Fred was ten, he had left the family home in Ohio to spend three months with his father in Illinois, where Grant was helping to train Union troops for war. Fred had begged to go along, and his father had consented. "I, being the eldest, was treated by him always as if I were already a man, and was permitted to do many things that would have been considered too dangerous for the other children," Fred said.

His mother supported Fred going. "I considered it a pleasant summer outing for both of them," Julia Grant wrote in her memoir. But when the

Fred is standing to the left of his mother in this formal portrait of the Grant family. The other children include, from left, Nellie, Jesse, and Ulysses, Jr.

war began in earnest and Grant received orders sending him to Missouri, he refused to take his son. "We may have some fighting to do, and he is too young to have the exposure of camp life," Grant wrote to Julia. She immediately wrote back, "Do not send him home; Alexander was no older when he accompanied Philip. Do keep him with you." Her letter, with its reference to the young Alexander the Great and his father, arrived too late, for Fred was already on his way back.

Now, a year and a half later in this spring of 1863, Fred was with his father once again. He had been thrilled when his parents allowed him to leave school and join the army at his father's headquarters on the Mississippi River fifty miles north of Vicksburg. This time Fred was determined not to be sent home. His goal was to be there when the guns of Vicksburg were finally silenced and the Mississippi River was totally in Union hands.

At the moment of surrender, Fred would be at his father's side, sharing sweet victory.

When he arrived onboard the ship that served as Grant's headquarters, his father greeted him warmly. He showed Fred the cabin they would share belowdecks. Grant's officers fussed over the boy. One gave him a personal tour of one of the ironclads—the most powerful fighting machines in the Union navy, with metal hulls that offered protection against gunfire. Another officer presented him with a pony. He even received a regulation army uniform that had been specially made for him. Fred was a handsome boy with his father's strong spirit. Dressed smartly in his uniform and sitting proudly on his pony, he accompanied the general on daily troop inspections.

Since his infancy Fred had been around soldiers, and he enjoyed their company. He quickly settled into life on the ship. Instead of dining with the officers, he ate most of his meals with the enlisted men. Many nights he left his father's cabin belowdecks to sleep up top where it was cool, soldiers stretched out all around him.

As happy as Fred was to be with the army, he was aware of the pressure on his father to finish the job he had come to do. Grant's inability to take control of the river was a topic of both speculation and derision throughout the North. Grant and his army of 33,000 men had joined Sherman and his nearly 30,000 men in January 1863, a few weeks after Sherman's defeat at Chickasaw Bayou. In the months since, Grant had sought a way to get his troops close enough to Vicksburg to attack. But each time he tried, either the Confederates or the Mississippi River sabotaged his plan. One plan had been to dig a canal that would create a new channel in the river, allowing ships to bypass Vicksburg and its guns. The men dug and dug, but the force of the river always destroyed their efforts, and finally Grant gave up.

He also tried to find an alternate water route to Vicksburg through the bayous and swamps that threaded off the river north of the city, but Union boats became trapped by trees that grew up through the murky, alligator-infested water. If a boat struck a tree—and it was impossible not to—lizards, raccoons, cockroaches, rats, and poisonous snakes fell out of the branches, sometimes landing on the boat's deck. Nervous sailors had to stand by with brooms to hastily brush them away. Even a few wildcats landed on boat decks and had to be shot. Confederate snipers onshore were yet another problem, for they dogged the boats, forcing sailors to stay belowdecks whenever possible.

When Fred arrived in Mississippi in early April, the weather was already hot. He saw for himself the toll the constant rain and slogging around in mud and muggy bayous had taken on the men. Young soldiers from states like Pennsylvania, Indiana, and New York were falling victim to pneumonia, malaria, and smallpox. Food was poor, the arrival of mail from home and paychecks from the government was undependable, and tempers grew thin.

The navy ironclads had their share of trouble, too. Confederates sank the Union *Cairo*—the first ship in naval history to be the victim of an electri-

The USS Cairo, *sunk by a Confederate mine, had thirteen heavy cannon and was covered with twelve inches of metal.*

cally detonated mine. After that, Union boats were more careful to sweep for mines before passing along the river.

Grant had other problems as well. Everywhere he went, Southern blacks left the homes and plantations where they had been slaves and followed the army, afraid for their safety if they struck out on their own, for in the eyes of most Southerners, they were not free. Grant was unsure what to do with them. As their numbers grew, feeding them became a burden. He employed some of them as laborers and cooks, but their numbers kept swelling.

Many black families escaped their masters and fled to the safety of Union lines. Grant had an estimated 10,000 liberated slaves with his army at Vicksburg.

Northern newspaper editors questioned everything. There was a war to fight, the troops were critically needed in other places, and here was the Army of the Tennessee still trying to silence the guns at Vicksburg. President Lincoln had selected Grant as the man to take Vicksburg because he knew Grant wouldn't give up. The president's confidence surprised some, for Grant had not yet proved himself to be an outstanding leader and had only a few victories to his credit. But Lincoln said of him, "I cannot spare this man. He fights."

Fred knew that his father's soldiers loved him. They not only followed him, they worked for him. Grant stood five feet, eight inches tall and weighed 140 pounds. He was a plain man, rumpled, not given to talking very much. He almost always had a cigar in his mouth, whether lit or unlit. Though he was only forty-one, the soldiers affectionately referred to him as "The Old Man." One said of him, "Somehow he was more partner than boss; we were in this thing together."

Grant's close friend General William Tecumseh Sherman was also "in this thing" with him. Sherman was forty-three, tall, craggy, with red hair and a scruffy red beard. Like Grant, he chain-smoked cigars, and he was restless, his hands always moving. When he was born, his father named him "Tecumseh" for the Shawnee Indian chief he considered a great war-

Sherman ably assisted Grant's efforts in the Vicksburg campaign.

rior. Sherman was still a boy when his father died, and other family members added the first name "William," feeling the child needed something more suitable. Sherman had been at West Point with Grant, and they had served in the Mexican War together. Their friendship was strong. They knew they could trust and rely on each other.

About the time Fred joined his father on the Mississippi, Grant was explaining to Sherman and his other officers his newest plan to take Vicksburg. Though it involved a long route to reach the town, after Grant's previous disasters it seemed the best way to actually get there.

But it was complicated. The army was currently in Louisiana, across the river and north of Vicksburg, so the first step would be to march the men south along the Louisiana shore—a slow, arduous task through difficult, often flooded terrain—to a point below Vicksburg.

Then navy ships, currently on the river north of the city with Grant, would make a run southward to try to get past Vicksburg's

Admiral David Porter, commander of the navy's Mississippi River squadron, had a reputation for acting alone, but he worked well in partnership with Grant.

guns. If the run past the batteries was successful, the ships would then transport the Union army, which would be waiting on the Louisiana shore, across the river and into Mississippi. Rather than try to fight through the swamps that protected Vicksburg to the south, Grant would march the men east to the state capital of Jackson, and then follow the Jackson road west back to Vicksburg. As the army surrounded and attacked the city, the Union navy would bombard it from the river. Once that happened, Grant was confident he could force Vicksburg's surrender within a day.

Grant's officers were skeptical. Though Sherman privately feared failure, he agreed to go along with the plan. Navy admiral David Dixon Porter, whose ironclads would take the brunt of fire if the fleet was discovered while trying to pass Vicksburg, viewed the plan with reluctance, but like Sherman, he trusted Grant. His ships would be ready.

As for Fred, he had no doubts. *This* plan was going to work!

✳ ✳ ✳

IN THE WEEKS THAT FOLLOWED, the army marched southward along the Louisiana shore, sometimes struggling through muck and bogs, until the men were finally south of Vicksburg. The next step was for the navy to transport them across the river and into the state of Mississippi. It was time to try to get the entire fleet, including the ship that served as Grant's headquarters, downriver beyond Vicksburg.

Grant was confident they could do it. He selected April 16 as the night for this venture. With luck, clouds would cover the moon, and, as the ships floated downriver in the darkness, the Confederates would never be the wiser. Fred planned to be standing right on deck with his father when they silently glided past Vicksburg.

During the day of April 16, as sailors busily prepared each boat for that night's run, Julia Grant arrived with her younger three children for a visit. She had managed to get a ride down the river from Memphis, where the family was staying, and had brought Ulysses Jr., who was ten, Nellie, seven, and little Jesse, just five, to visit their older brother and their father. Grant was pleased to see them. No sooner had they arrived than Fred heard his mother offering his father suggestions on how to take Vicksburg. Julia Grant recalled that, in response to her unsolicited advice, "the General was greatly amused and inquired if I, too, had a plan of action to propose. Of course I had."

While she was explaining it, Grant's eyes twinkled. Then he said, "Mrs. Grant, I will move upon Vicksburg and will take it, too. You need give yourself no further trouble . . . I am glad you arrived in time to witness the running of the blockade." He explained how that night the Union ships would "drop silently down the river as far as possible and then put on all steam and go flying past Vicksburg and its batteries to where I want to use them."

Julia Grant was delighted. She had been at Holly Springs with Grant the previous December when the Union supply base was raided and destroyed by Confederate troops. Her carriage had been burned and her horses stolen, but she took danger in stride and looked forward to the evening's events.

In Vicksburg that April day, the air was filled with the scent of blooming flowers. Though daily life had not changed much for most people, the town had been transformed into a fortress. General Pemberton now had 172 cannon and 30,000 troops in place along a semicircle of military fortifications surrounding Vicksburg. Sentries along the riverfront kept a close eye on the water, and the cannon were loaded and ready. The Yankees had been in the area for months, and as far as the people of Vicksburg were concerned, all they'd managed to do was dig an ill-fated canal and try various silly schemes in the bayous where their boats got stuck. Surely they were about to leave for good and go back north. But until that actually happened, no one was going to take chances.

By sundown, Grant was ready. The waters of the mighty Mississippi were calm and black as ink, and soon the sky would be as well. The Union fleet included seven gunboats, one steam ram, three transports full of supplies, and an assortment of smaller boats. The bigger boats had bales of hay and cotton and sacks of grain stacked up on deck to protect the boilers, which could blow up if hit by enemy fire. The ironclads had coal barges strapped to their sides to give them extra protection. The boats would travel with no lights and move at low speed. Those with few or no guns, which included Grant's, would hug the Louisiana shore, protected by Porter's ironclads. If they were spotted, the ironclads were prepared for a fight.

The sky lit up like daylight the night when Grant's fleet made its successful run past the batteries at Vicksburg.

Several of Grant's officers had their wives and children with them, and the families dined together aboard Grant's headquarters ship. By ten p.m. everyone was on deck and ready. It was almost as if they were waiting for the curtain to open on a play. The adults were drinking champagne. Grant smoked a cigar, and he and Julia sat in chairs, holding hands, their children around them. Fred could clearly see his father's face, calm and relaxed as he watched first one navy vessel and then another begin the silent glide toward the Vicksburg waterfront.

Suddenly the Vicksburg cannon opened fire, exploding in the night sky like the Fourth of July. Lookouts had spotted the fleet. They hurriedly set fire to several abandoned houses along the Louisiana shore, illuminating the river and giving the cannon better aim at the advancing ships. The ironclads returned fire, aiming at the Vicksburg guns but also hurtling shells into the town, where they exploded with fiery howls. Several buildings went up in flames, and people sixty miles away could hear the explosions.

Onboard his father's ship, Fred gripped the railing with anticipation as he watched the bombardment, exhilarated by the sounds and sights and the thunderous roar of the multitude of explosions. One of the ships was hit, caught fire, and slowly began to sink. Fred breathed a sigh of relief when he saw the sailors who had jumped into the river being rescued by another boat.

With all the gunfire and the burning ship, "the river was lighted up as if by sunlight," Fred observed. When he focused his spyglass on Vicksburg, he saw residents running through the streets. He watched as some headed to higher ground where they could get a clear view of the river, and noted that "the people of Vicksburg lined the hills, and manifested great excitement."

"Indeed, it was a grand sight," Julia Grant wrote in her memoir. "How vividly that picture is photographed on my mind; the grand roar of the cannon rests in my memory. The batteries of Vicksburg poured shot and shell upon the heads of the devoted little fleet, but Porter was there–thank Heaven!–to return broadside for broadside. The air was full of sulphurous smoke."

For nearly two hours Fred watched the battle with his family as their boat slowly made its way downriver. During the entire time, he would remember that his father "was quietly smoking, but an intense light shone in his eyes." Years later Grant himself wrote in his memoir that the sights that night were "magnificent, but terrible," while an officer with him said, "It was as if hell itself were loose that night on the Mississippi River."

And then it was over. When the last boat made it past the Vicksburg waterfront, cannon on both sides ceased fire and the battle stopped as quickly as it had begun. Grant had lost only one ship: the rest had safely run the gauntlet and were now south of the city. In the wee hours of the morning onboard Grant's ship, Julia Grant noted, "The batteries were passed, and we rested here awaiting the report of casualties and were happy to learn that there had been no loss of life, although some few were wounded–poor fellows! The smoke cleared away, the stars looked down tenderly upon Union and Rebel alike, and the katydids and the frogs began again their summer songs."

Now if all went as planned, General Ulysses Grant would soon storm Vicksburg, his young son at his side, and once and for all destroy the guns guarding the Mississippi.

BURYING THE FAMILY SILVER

Late Spring 1863

That terrible night of April 16, when the Union fleet was passing the waterfront and the first explosions rocked Vicksburg, the Reverend W. W. Lord and his wife, Margaret, had leaped from their bed. Their five children were already wide awake, terrified by the noise. The Lords hurriedly gathered the children and, with the help of their two frightened house slaves, urged everyone out of the house, across the lawn, and into the church next door. Guided only by candles, they felt their way into the small, windowless basement coal bin, where Dr. Lord hastily spread rugs and blankets over the lumpy coal. There they stayed for the next two hours, trying to shut out the awful sounds of exploding shells.

The Reverend W. W. Lord was rector of Christ Church in Vicksburg from 1854 to 1863.

Eleven-year-old Willie—whose given name was William Wilberforce Lord, Jr.—quickly realized that they were in real danger. These Yankee guns were more powerful than the last ones, and shells were landing higher in the city. Willie had been excited by all the war preparations in Vicksburg and, along with his friends, had eagerly followed the activity of the Union fleet on the river. The possibility of war had seemed like a fairy tale to him. But tonight was different. "With the deep but muffled boom of the guns reaching us at intervals in our underground retreat, my mother and sisters huddled around me upon the coal-heap," he later recalled. "Lighted by the fitful glow of two or three tallow candles, the war became to me for the first time a reality."

The Lords were from New York but had lived in Vicksburg for ten years. Dr. Lord was the minister of Christ Episcopal Church, high in the hills of the city, and his large congregation included many of Vicksburg's most prominent citizens. Margaret Lord was a high-strung woman who worried constantly, but Dr. Lord had determined that, in spite of the danger, they would not leave Vicksburg. Not only was it their home, but he supported the South in this war. In addition to his church duties, he served as chaplain for the First Mississippi Brigade of the Confederate Army. He was well educated—a graduate of Princeton Theological Seminary—and a published poet. He was reputed to have one of the largest private libraries in the South, and his books occupied every wall in his study. Willie shared his father's love of learning and sometimes read aloud to his sisters from *Robinson Crusoe* and his other favorite adventure tales.

But this night of the bombardment, books and learning seemed far away. There was nothing to do but wait, and pray, and hope for the best.

✳ ✳ ✳

ELSEWHERE IN VICKSBURG, the first thunderous boom of the cannon along the waterfront had jolted people out of sleep. The Union fleet trying to sneak down the river was returning fire, hurling shell after shell into the town. China cabinets rattled, dogs howled, and horses spooked as the black sky filled with smoke and flashes of light. The odor of gunpowder filled the air, and candles and lanterns lit up every house. People ran out of their homes in confusion, then rushed back inside. Should they stay? Seek shelter in one of the new caves scattered about? Was there time to harness horses and flee? Some went to Sky Parlor Hill, where they gasped in horror at the sight of the battle raging on the river.

Not far from the hill and close to Christ Episcopal Church, twenty-seven-year-old Mary Loughborough (pronounced "Lof-burrow") was experiencing the horrors of that night. Her husband, James, was an officer in the Confederate army and was stationed at Vicksburg. Mary lived in Jackson, forty miles away, and had left their two-year-old daughter with friends there so she could come by train earlier that day to visit her husband. When she arrived in Vicksburg, she was surprised to see the damage in the city from the previous shelling and had commented to her friend, "How is it possible you live here?" Her friend responded, "After one is accustomed to the change, we do not mind. But becoming accustomed, that is the trial."

As Mary had settled into her hosts' home with its view of the river,

James Loughborough.

Mary Loughborough.

she wrote in her diary, "I looked over this beautiful landscape, and in the distance plainly saw the Federal transports lying quietly at their anchorage. Was it a dream? Could I believe that over this smiling scene in the bright April morning the blight of civil warfare lay like a pall?"

That evening Mary and her husband took a carriage ride through the streets of Vicksburg. Later they sat on their friends' veranda to enjoy the balmy night air. Mary found herself studying the river through her spyglass, watching the Union ships anchored north of the city. Finally she put the glass away and prepared for bed. But she could not stop thinking about the enemy fleet. "Resting in Vicksburg," she noted, "seemed like resting near a volcano."

When the shelling started, Mary awoke instantly. "I sprang from my bed, drew on my slippers and robe, and went out on the veranda . . . The river was illuminated by large fires on the bank, and we could discern plainly the huge, black masses floating down with the current, now and then belching forth fire from their sides . . . and we could hear the shells exploding in the upper part of town . . . We could hear the gallop, in the darkness, of couriers upon the paved streets; we could hear the voices of the soldiers on the riverside. The rapid firing from the boats, the roar of the Confederate batteries, and, above all, the screaming, booming sound of the shells, as they exploded in the air and around the city, made at once a new and fearful scene to me."

Mary's husband had to report immediately to his regiment. As he was leaving, he urged her to seek shelter in their hosts' backyard cave. "While I hesitated," Mary recalled, ". . . a shell exploded near the side of the house. Fear instantly decided me and I ran, guided by one of the ladies, who pointed down the steep slope of the hill . . . While I was considering the best way of descending the hill, another shell exploded . . . I flew down, half sliding and running. Before I had reached the mouth of the cave, two more exploded on the side of the hill near me. Breathless and terrified, I found the entrance and ran in, having left one of my slippers on the hillside.

"Shell after shell fell in the valley below us, exploding with a loud, rumbling noise, perfectly deafening. The cave was an excavation in the earth the size of a large room, high enough for the tallest person to stand perfectly erect, provided with comfortable seats, and altogether quite a large and habitable abode . . . were it not for the dampness and the constant contact with the soft earthy walls."

When the shelling stopped after two impossibly long hours, Mary and the others cautiously emerged, shaken but safe. They watched the river as the one Union boat that had been hit by Confederate fire slowly burned and sank. "We remained on the veranda an hour or more, the gentlemen speculating on the result of the successful run by the batteries," Mary reported. "All were astonished and chagrined."

The next day townspeople watched in disbelief as Union troops set up two large cannon on the Louisiana shore, directly across from the Vicksburg waterfront, and opened fire. A few shells reached land, and once again the earth rumbled and exploded.

Mary's only thought was to get back to her little daughter in Jackson. At the station, where several shells had already fallen, she waited anxiously for the train to arrive. Finally "the glad sound of the whistle was heard, and, after our long suspense, we felt the motion of the cars again, and were glad to leave Vicksburg, with the sound of the cannon and noise of the shell still ringing in our ears."

✳ ✳ ✳

GRANT'S SUCCESS shook the little city to its very core. Townspeople had felt secure, even invincible. But with the Yankee fleet now below Vicksburg, they realized that Grant could easily transport his army across the river and would then be in a strong position to attack.

Knowing how risky it was to remain in Vicksburg, Willie's parents faced a difficult decision. Dr. Lord was determined to stay to care for his congregation. But when word arrived from a friend who owned a large plantation a few miles outside town that the family was welcome to come there, he and his wife decided that she and the children should go. The next day, according to Willie, "our entire household, excepting only my father . . . departed for Flowers' plantation near the Big Black River, where shelter and entertainment had been offered us in anticipation of the shelling of the city. Our most valued household effects, including my father's library . . . followed us in a canvas covered army wagon." Margaret Lord was from a wealthy family, and the wagon also carried her beautiful clothes, along with valuable rugs, mirrors, paintings, and other household furnishings. Before leaving Vicksburg, she had the house slaves bury the heavy family silver in the churchyard.

At the Flowers plantation, the Lords received, in Willie's words, "a planter's cordial welcome . . . Here we were most pleasantly domiciled, to remain undisturbed, as my father hoped, as long as the siege should last."

✳ ✳ ✳

LUCY'S FAMILY also sought refuge outside Vicksburg. The day after the Federal troops ran past the blockade, her parents decided that her father would stay behind so he could look after business interests, while her mother would take the children to the comfortable home they owned just outside the small town of Bolton's Depot, thirty miles from Vicksburg. Like the Lords, they took along their most valuable household furniture and treasures for safekeeping. Their slaves, Rice and Mary Ann, went with them.

Whatever the task, Rice obediently did what he was told, but Lucy could see his growing reluctance. She didn't believe for a moment that Yankees would *ever* set foot in Vicksburg, but they *were* nearby, and lots of slaves were running away from their masters to find refuge with the Union troops and claim their freedom.

How would her family ever get along if Rice left them? And what would he do if he were free?

AT THE BATTLE FRONT

Late Spring 1863

When Fred woke up the morning of May 1, his father was not in the cabin the two of them shared belowdecks, nor could Fred find him anywhere on the ship. General Lorenzo Thomas, who was in charge, told him that Grant had gone to Port Gibson, eight miles away, and that "I was to remain where I was until he came back." That was an order. Fred could get no more information from him.

The Union army was now on Mississippi soil, twenty miles south of Vicksburg. The first thing Grant wanted to do was to secure the river coast for the Federals by seizing control of Grand Gulf and Port Gibson, both Confederate strongholds. Two days earlier, on April 29, Admiral Porter's ironclads had tried to take Grand Gulf but had failed. As Fred now knew, today his father was attacking Port Gibson.

Fred stood at the ship's railing, watching all the activity around him. Onshore he saw troops preparing to march in the direction of the cannon fire he could hear in the distance.

He knew what he had to do. He respected his father, and he strived to be a good soldier and obey orders. But he could not wait out the battle here onboard ship. He *had* to go.

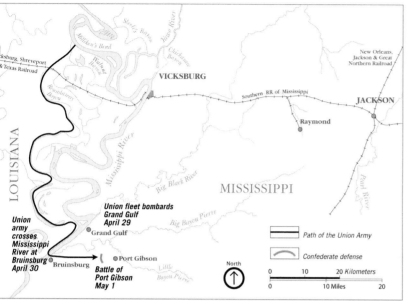

VICKSBURG

JACKSON

Raymond

MISSISSIPPI

LOUISIANA

New Orleans, Jackson & Great Northern Railroad

Southern RR of Mississippi

Vicksburg, Shreveport & Texas Railroad

Big Black River

Big Bayou Pierre

Union fleet bombards Grand Gulf April 29

Grand Gulf

Union army crosses Mississippi River at Bruinsburg April 30

Bruinsburg

Port Gibson

Battle of Port Gibson May 1

Little Bayou Pierre

North

Path of the Union Army

Confederate defense

0   10   20 Kilometers

0   10 Miles   20

Porter's ships, now successfully downstream from Vicksburg, transported Grant's army across the Mississippi River at Bruinsburg on April 30. The following day Grant attacked the Confederates at Port Gibson.

He saw his chance when a rabbit onshore caught his eye. All innocence, "I asked General Thomas to let me go ashore and catch the rabbit."

The unsuspecting Thomas gave permission, and moments later Fred was onshore and running. He caught up to a wagon train and was able to ride one of the mules for a while before marching with an artillery group and then a regiment. The whole time the sounds of battle were coming closer.

Fred didn't describe what happened next, but soldiers often felt overwhelmed and confused by their first taste of battle. Fred may have been momentarily deafened by the roar of cannon, or even knocked to his knees when the ground shook from the thunderous blasts. It is hard to imagine what he must have felt as the air became hazy with smoke and he heard the sounds of gunfire and the shouts and cries of his comrades, some falling under fire.

He did report that he eventually spotted his father on his horse watching the unfolding scene. He wanted to go to him, he recalled, but "my guilty conscience so troubled me that I hid from his sight behind a tree."

When he thought it was not possible for the battle to last another minute, the Union troops, who greatly outnumbered the Rebels, finally got the upper hand. As they rushed forward, the sun already beginning to set, Fred joined the shouts of "Hurrah!" for "the enemy had given way."

He ran onto the battlefield among the exhausted, jubilant men, cheering, but as the celebration began to die down and he looked around, he was suddenly sobered. Fallen soldiers were everywhere, some dead, some dying, many begging for help. This would not have been his first time seeing casualties: two days earlier, after the battle for Grand Gulf, he had seen

sailors on the ironclads who had been killed or injured and it had sickened him. Now, at Port Gibson, "the horrors of a battlefield were brought vividly before me," he said. "Night came on and I walked among our men in the moonlight." Though dazed, he realized that all about him, soldiers who were uninjured were helping with the dead and wounded. "I followed four soldiers who were carrying a dead man in a blanket. They put the body down a slope of a little hill among a dozen other bodies. The sight made me faint . . . and I hurried on."

Wanting to help, he joined a detachment that was transporting the wounded to a schoolhouse that served as a field hospital. He was unprepared for what he saw next. "Surgeons were tossing amputated arms and legs out of the windows. The yard of the schoolhouse was filled with wounded and groaning men who were waiting for the surgeons."

Twelve-year-old Fred could take no more. "I picked my way among

Doctors and nurses traveled with the armies to care for the wounded at field hospitals like this one behind Union lines.

Though he commanded an army, Grant shared the same living conditions as ordinary soldiers.

them to the side of the road and sat on the roots of a tree. I was hungry, thirsty and worn out, and, worse than all, I didn't know if my father were living or dead. No boy was ever more utterly wretched."

Then a man on horseback stopped and looked down at him, exclaiming, "Why, hello, is that really you?" It was one of his father's officers, and Fred was greatly relieved to see him. "Dismounting, he proceeded to make me comfortable, putting down his saddle for a pillow, and advising me to go to sleep. This I did, but my sleep was broken by dreams of the horrors I had witnessed."

Later, the officer awoke him to tell him General Grant had arrived. Through exhausted eyes, Fred looked where the officer pointed. "About fifty yards off sat my father, drinking coffee from a tin cup. I went to him, and was greeted with an exclamation of surprise, as he supposed I was still on board the boat."

Grant was direct. "How did you get here?"

"I walked," Fred confessed, certain he was in trouble. But his father surprised him. "He looked at me for a moment, and then said, 'I guess you will do.' And there was no anger in his face. Maybe I was mistaken, but I half believed he was not sorry that I left the gunboat."

The next morning, as the army broke camp, he managed to find a horse to ride. It had no harness, but he was able to make one from some rope he found on the ground. All day he followed the troops. His father had gone somewhere else, and he was on his own. When the troops stopped for the night, he sought shelter at a house "where some officers were sleeping on a porch. I crawled in for a nap between two of them." The next day when he joined his father, Grant noticed that Fred's horse was lame. "Father, who was ever kind and thoughtful, insisted that I should take his mount."

During the next week, Grant was able to claim another victory, for Federal troops took possession of Grand Gulf when retreating Confederates abandoned it after their loss at Port Gibson. One day, while the Union army rested, Fred and a young orderly were exploring some of the countryside when they saw a house with a dozen horses tied up in front. Hoping for some glory, "we conceived the idea of capturing the mounts, and possibly the riders also, who were inside the house. Not until we had gone too far to retreat did the idea occur to us that the would-be captors might possibly become the captured.

"It was with great relief that we saw a man wearing a blue uniform come out of the house, and we then discovered that the party we had proposed to capture was a detachment of Sherman's signal corps."

✻ ✻ ✻

A WEEK LATER, the army started moving northeast toward the state capital of Jackson, sixty miles away. Grant's plan was to defeat Confederate general Joe Johnston, whose army occupied the city, so Johnston couldn't help defend Vicksburg. Once Grant was in control of Jackson, he would march his army back west toward Vicksburg, taking advantage of the good road that stretched the forty miles between the two cities.

The Mississippi weather slowed the troops as they moved toward Jackson. It rained every day, soaking the men as they trudged along muddy roads. Wagons got stuck, and fires were hard to start and harder to keep

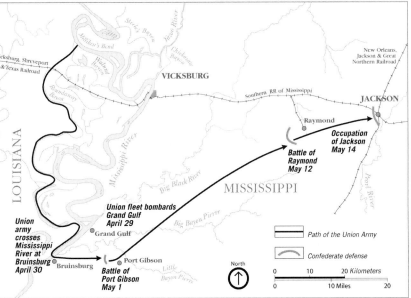

MISSISSIPPI

LOUISIANA

VICKSBURG

JACKSON

Raymond

Occupation
of Jackson
May 14

Battle of
Raymond
May 12

Union fleet bombards
Grand Gulf
April 29

Union
army
crosses
Mississippi
River at
Bruinsburg
April 30

Grand Gulf

Bruinsburg

Port Gibson

Battle of
Port Gibson
May 1

North

Path of the Union Army

Confederate defense

0   10   20 Kilometers

0   10 Miles   20

Grant defeated the Confederates at Raymond on May 12 before marching on to Jackson.

going. So his army could move more quickly, Grant had brought along only basic supplies. He had learned early on that food was abundant enough in the agricultural South that his army could live off the land—or at least it could while plantations were still intact and fully stocked. That was changing. But on the march to Jackson he expected the men to scavenge for food. Fred found meals with his father to be so irregular that "I, for one, did not propose to put up with such living, and I took my meals with the soldiers, who did a little foraging, and thereby set an infinitely better table than their commanding general. My father's table at this time was, I must frankly say, the worst I ever saw or partook of."

General Grant slept on the ground with his men, "without a tent, in the midst of his soldiers, with his saddle for a pillow and without even an overcoat for covering," according to a newspaper reporter traveling with the troops. The reporter went on to write, "More than one night, I bivouacked on the ground in the rain after being all day in my saddle. The most comfortable night I had, in fact, was in a church of which the officers had taken possession. Having no pillow, I went up to the pulpit and borrowed the Bible for the night."

Grant was certain he wouldn't make it all the way to Jackson without a challenge from the Rebels. It came on May 12 when advance Union troops approached Raymond, Mississippi. The Confederates were waiting for them and opened fire. Neither side knew the size of the opposing force, though it would gradually become clear that the Rebels, with 3,000 men, were outnumbered three to one. The fighting was savage. Sometimes the two sides were so close to each other, they used their guns as clubs because it was too crowded to aim and shoot.

50 UNDER SIEGE!

More Federal troops arrived, but the Confederates held on. Finally, badly outnumbered, they fell back through the little town of Raymond. It was raining. Women in the town were caring for wounded men, protecting them from the rain with quilts they had brought from home. In anticipation of a Confederate victory, they had also fixed a grand meal for their soldiers. But hungry as they were, the retreating Rebels dared not stop to eat. Instead, the Yankees pursuing them stopped just long enough to gulp down the food.

Fred was not at the Battle of Raymond, but he arrived there the next day with his father, "and here again I saw the horrors of war, the wounded and the unburied dead." He no longer had any illusions about the grandiosity of war: the price the men paid was terrible.

Though the rain never let up, the Union army resumed its march toward Jackson. Bands of Rebel guerrillas dogged them, their sharpshooters keeping Union soldiers on edge. Both Grant and Sherman fought in skirmishes, often leading the action. Fred remembered one incident when "the enemy's sharpshooters opened fire on us. One of the staff

Because of all the smoke and dust, commanders on both sides had problems sizing up each other at the Battle of Raymond.

Rebel guerrillas, like this legendary group known as Mosby's Raiders, bedeviled Union troops as they moved through the South.

shouted to my father that they were aiming at him. His answer was to turn his horse and dash into the woods in the direction whence the bullets were coming." Grant's staff quickly followed, and together they pushed back the Rebels.

When the army finally reached the outskirts of Jackson, Fred left his father's side and pressed ahead on his own. He hoped to take possession of the Rebel flag flying from the state capitol and keep it as a souvenir. "Confederate troops passed me in their retreat," he said. "Though I wore a blue uniform, I was so splashed with mud, and looked generally so unattractive, that the Confederates paid no attention to me."

In pounding rain, Fred rode into the city and encountered "a mounted officer with a Union flag advancing toward the capitol." Fred followed. When he saw the capitol building, he raced ahead into its now-deserted halls, intent on only one thing. But he was too late—another Union soldier had already claimed the prized Rebel flag. Still, he proudly stood at attention when the American flag was raised above the building to take its place, and he was there to greet his father when Grant later rode into town.

Arriving Union troops had expected a fight from General Joe Johnston and his Confederate army. But Johnston had fled and it took only five hours on May 14 for the Union bluecoats to spread out and occupy the city, fighting small groups of holdout insurgents as they went. Grant ordered Sherman to destroy anything that could contribute to the Confederate cause. As a result, much of the city was burned to the ground. Fred was with General Sherman and said, "I saw the match put to the stores of baled cotton, at my father's order."

With factories and warehouses destroyed and the rail lines cut, Grant had struck a severe blow to Mississippi's war effort. He was now between the armies of the Confederate generals Joe Johnston and John Pemberton, and he was on solid land, only forty miles from Vicksburg. All that remained was to march west and take the city. Then, finally, he could silence the cannon guarding the river and bring that great waterway under Union control.

When Grant and Sherman entered Jackson, they stopped at a textile mill. Grant allowed the workers time to gather their belongings and then burned the mill.

Before fleeing the city, General Johnston had been quartered in the best room at the Bowman House, Jackson's finest hotel. That night of May 14, after two weeks on the road, General Grant slept in a bed at last— the very one Joe Johnston had occupied the night before.

THE YANKEES ARE COMING!

May 1863

After enduring the shelling of Vicksburg the night of April 16, when Grant successfully got his ships down the river, Mary Loughborough had been happy to stay at home in Jackson with her little daughter. She felt safe there, for the city was protected by Joe Johnston and his army. Then the news came: Grant was headed toward Jackson and would soon attack! Not only that, but there would be no defense. General Johnston had ordered Jackson evacuated. He and his troops were leaving.

Reeling in shock, people wondered where to go. What place was safe? The Yankees were everywhere!

Mary tried not to panic. She was responsible for the safety of her daughter and her two house slaves. An occupying army wasn't her greatest fear: "We were in far more danger here from the rabble that usually followed a large army, and who might plunder, insult, and rob us," she said.

She sought advice from friends. One who was leaving immediately for Vicksburg by train urged her to come, too. Mary hesitated, thinking, "May I not be in danger in Vicksburg? Suppose the gunboats should make an attack?" But her husband was in Vicksburg, and she wanted to be near him.

"Very hurriedly we made our arrangements, packing with scarcely a moment to lose, not stopping to discuss our sudden move and the alarming news." The streets of Jackson were jammed with wagons, carriages, and people on foot. Panicked citizens rushed in all directions. When Mary and her daughter, slaves, and friends finally reached the train depot, it "was crowded with crushing and elbowing human beings, swaying to and fro—baggage being thrown hither and thither—horses wild with fright . . . and so we found ourselves in a car, amid the living stream that flowed and surged along . . . seeking anything to bear them away from the threatened and fast depopulating town."

The little group managed to get seats, and soon the train was chugging through the countryside with its cargo of refugees. When the train pulled into Vicksburg that evening, the depot was crowded with soldiers heading out to fight. Mary was greatly relieved to see her husband, who had come to the station, hoping she would be on the train from Jackson. He took her to the home of friends and assured her that she had made the right decision.

But the next morning she was upset to learn that General Pemberton was urging everyone but soldiers to leave, for it was clear, now that Grant had reached Jackson, that he would soon march on Vicksburg. Mary thought briefly of trying to find a place in the country. But the Yankees were out there. The city, on the other hand, was guarded by Confederate troops. When her husband assured her that Pemberton would meet Grant miles from town and soundly defeat him, she decided to stay.

The next few days were uneventful. "With our sewing in the morning, and rides in the evening, our home was very pleasant—very happy and quiet." Each day she visited Sky Parlor Hill and peered through her spyglass at the Union gunboats that stayed just out of reach of the Vicksburg cannon. Federal troops were encamped along the Louisiana shore directly across from the Vicksburg wharf. Watching them, she said, was "far more stirring and interesting than the quiet fortified life of Vicksburg."

✻ ✻ ✻

BUT THE CALM did not last. All of Vicksburg was horrified to learn that the Yankees had burned Jackson and that they were laying waste to the countryside. Grant's men seemed bent on total destruction. They tore up railroad tracks, pulled down telegraph lines, burned cotton fields— anything they could do to demoralize citizens and cripple the South's ability to fight. They killed poultry and livestock; emptied crocks of molasses and vinegar; and burned homes, smokehouses, barns, stores, and warehouses. Horses, mules, oxen, carriages, and wagons were confiscated for the army's use. In spite of orders to the contrary, many officers looked the other way when soldiers stole jewelry, china, and silver; slashed feather mattresses; and took clothing. Though army rules forbade it, some officers claimed valuable belongings for themselves.

Stories of looting and destruction spread quickly. The cry of "The Yankees are coming!" struck fear into every heart. Southerners thought these men must be cutthroat monsters, more animal than human. In fear of their lives, many people hid when the Yankees approached, leaving their valuables unguarded. A Union officer told of houses that were grand beyond description, and how the owners had run off, leaving his men to help themselves.

One young girl, whose family had fled Vicksburg to hide on a plantation, watched in fear as Yankee soldiers marched along the road. She saw that "their arms were filled with fine china, plates, dishes, and every kind of ware, which they had taken from the Blackman place adjoining our plantation. As they rode along they would throw these beautiful pieces to the ground just for the pastime of seeing them smashed to a thousand pieces."

A Union soldier wrote home that he'd seen forty or fifty plantations burn in a single day. Before setting them afire, officers often quartered in them for one or more nights. General Grant himself was known to enter kitchens and order whoever still lived there to feed his officers. Usually it was only old people, women, and children who remained, for older boys and men were in the Confederate army. A few slaves continued to serve their owners, but most left the moment the Yankees appeared. It wasn't just

Union soldiers terrorizing the population. Blacks following the army did their share of looting and tried to carry their newfound treasures with them, even if it meant dragging along furniture, rugs, and featherbeds.

※ ※ ※

EVEN THOUGH THEY MISSED THEIR FATHER, who had stayed in Vicksburg to continue his ministry, Willie Lord and his sisters were happy at the Flowers plantation, deep in the countryside. They had plenty of space to play, and the plantation house was most interesting to explore.

But Mrs. Lord worried. She missed her husband and complained about being separated from him. When rumors reached the plantation that

Southerners had to decide whether to stay and try to protect their property, or take what they could and flee. Many lost everything, regardless of which choice they made.

In the agricultural South, some plantation owners had thousands of acres of land, hundreds of slaves, and large, beautiful mansions. But most plantations were more like medium-sized farms, with fewer slaves and homes like the one shown here.

Yankees were in the area, she was convinced she and her children would be killed. "My mother was so constituted that when separated from those she loved, her imagination constantly drew the most painfully realistic pictures of possible disaster," said Willie. Mr. Flowers tried to assure her that she and her children were safe where they were, but she sent word to her husband, begging to come home. Willie knew that his father was concerned about the impact that worry was having on her health, and he "reluctantly gave his consent to our return to the city."

Soon preparations were in place. "On our return journey to Vicksburg we rode in state in the Flowers' family carriage," said Willie, "but left behind us, alas! the priceless library, our household bric-a-brac, and the greater part of my mother's dainty wardrobe; all, by the courteous permission of our host, stored, safely, as we supposed, in the apartments we had occupied on the ground floor of the plantation mansion. As it happened, this was about the worst possible disposal of our treasures."

The Lord family had just set out for Vicksburg when they received word that the Yankees had indeed arrived in the area and were burning and looting homes. What was meant to be a pleasant ride back home turned into a long and frightening journey, for they were fearful that at any moment the Yankees might catch them. Finally, with great relief, they came within sight of the city and soon reached their house. They found sleeping soldiers overflowing the church, and military wagons and artillery jamming the streets and filling the yard.

But they were home, and as long as Mrs. Lord had anything to say about it, they would not leave again.

✳ ✳ ✳

FOR SEVERAL WEEKS, Lucy and her mother and brothers had been content in their country home near the little town of Bolton's Depot. "My mother, so comfortably fixed . . . considered herself safe," Lucy said. But that all changed when they learned that Bolton's Depot was in the direct path of the Union army: "Suddenly one day," remembered Lucy, "there flashed through the town the news, *the Yankees are coming!*" Fearing for her family's lives, Indiana McRae determined that they must return immediately to Vicksburg. She hastily packed, ordering Rice to have the surrey and a wagon "ready to make an early start for Vicksburg tomorrow morning."

When Rice asked what was going on, Lucy's mother was reluctant to inform him, for she desperately needed his help and feared he would run away. When she did finally tell him, Lucy recalled, "I remember so well how the man almost rebelled, so anxious was he to get to the Federal army. I can see how fine and faithful he was to obey his mistress, when every fiber in his heart was crying out for that freedom."

Rice loaded all the trunks and household possessions he could fit into the wagon. Everything else had to be left behind. Early the next morning they started out. Rice drove the wagon, while Lucy, her mother and brothers, and their other slave, Mary Ann, followed behind, crowded into a surrey.

For ten-year-old Lucy, their journey that day was the adventure of a lifetime. As frightened as she was, she was caught up in the drama unfolding before her eyes. "When we drove into the little village of Bolton's Depot, all was confusion," she related. "Confederate cavalry and infantry were grouped about. To my young eyes this was exciting beyond expression, and right close did we children huddle to mother as she sat in the surrey, driving as fast as our heavy loads permitted. She inquired as to news, and the reply that the Yankees were close on us caused her much alarm.

"Mother kept Rice ahead with his heavy load, and our progress was slow. I shall never forget how my heart would beat as they talked of the Yankees being so close behind us. I do not know what I thought they were, but it was certainly something very dreadful. We pushed on, being stopped here and there and questioned. When we reached the Joe Davis place, belonging to the brother of the President, we found the plantation deserted . . . In answer to our request for water, a negro woman told us she was looking for the army every minute. Mother said, 'Drive on, Rice,' but Rice was not eager to go. Mother was constantly saying, 'Drive on, Rice, or they will catch us.' On our journey we could hear the roaring of cannon, and afterwards knew it was the Battle of Champion's Hill."

After long hours on a road jammed with horses, wagons, and carriages also fleeing toward Vicksburg, they finally reached the city. According to Lucy, with great relief they found that "there were no pickets along the road, no guards to ask questions, and we drove right on into town."

THE ROAD TO VICKSBURG

May 15–19, 1863

On May 15, Grant and most of his army departed Jackson, leaving the city in flames. Fred rode with his father. Everyone was tense, uncertain of what lay before them on the road to Vicksburg. The constant rain, the muddy roads, and the harsh hot sun slowed Grant's army. Northerners who had been in Mississippi since the beginning of Grant's campaign were becoming toughened to the heat and humidity, but newer troops, used to cool breezes, struggled to keep up.

The army stopped for the night, then was on the road early the next morning when spies confirmed that Pemberton was moving eastward toward them with 22,000 men. Grant, heading west, had 30,000 men. Even with greater troop strength, he expected a tough fight against Pemberton. They had served together in the Mexican War, and Grant knew that Pemberton was smart, strong, and disciplined. "This I thought of all the time he was in Vicksburg and I outside of it; and I knew he would hold on to the last," Grant later wrote.

Pemberton also knew a hard fight was ahead. His spies had reported Grant's troop strength, and he immediately regretted having left 10,000 of his men behind in Vicksburg—something he had to do in case the Yankees attacked from the river. He had expected to meet up with General Joe Johnston and merge their two armies, knowing that together they would outnumber the Federals. But where was Old Joe? Pemberton had received no word from him since Johnston had abandoned Jackson several days earlier.

Pemberton had other problems as well. He and his generals disagreed on strategy for the upcoming battle. Also, because Pemberton was a Northerner, some of the troops did not trust his leadership. He was from Philadelphia, and two of his brothers were Union officers. His wealthy family had disowned him when he decided to fight for the South—a decision influenced by his beautiful young wife, Patty, who was from Virginia and was passionately pro-Confederate.

Fortunately for Pemberton, all his generals and their men were united in their determination to beat the Yankees, even if they had to do it without Joe Johnston's help.

General John Pemberton.

Patty Pemberton.

On May 16, Grant's and Pemberton's armies met halfway between Jackson and Vicksburg on a farm belonging to the Champion family and began lining up opposite each other. The land included a high hill that became the center of what would be known as the Battle of Champion's Hill–the fiercest and most bloody battle of the Vicksburg campaign.

In the bloody Battle of Champion's Hill, when soldiers ran out of ammunition, they fixed their bayonets and charged.

On that morning, Grant was in high spirits, confident the day would end in victory. He called out to his men that this was the day they would fight the battle that would win Vicksburg. On a signal from officers, the battle began. Cannon roared their opening volleys and the two sides charged each other, then regrouped and charged again. Generals usually stayed far enough behind the front lines to be out of the range of fire, but on this day Grant stayed close to the men, riding up and down the lines on his horse, shouting orders, and encouraging and inspiring his troops.

Fred witnessed his father's bravery during a crucial moment. "Our line broke and was falling back when Father moved forward and rallied the men. He rode to all parts of the field, giving orders to the generals, and dispatching his staff in all directions." Appreciative soldiers fought hard for their commander. Many later reported seeing him on the battlefield, and several commented on his humbleness and his encouragement to the men, who always cheered when they saw him.

Both sides gave their all. When they were the attackers, the Confederates often employed their famed Rebel yell, meant to terrorize the bluecoats. One Union soldier described it as sounding like 10,000 starving and howling wolves.

Pemberton and his officers kept watching for Joe Johnston to join the battle, but Johnston didn't come. Finally, after a long and bloody day, the Union, with its superior numbers, forced the Confederates to withdraw in defeat.

✻ ✻ ✻

NIGHT FELL. Bill Aspinwall, a Union soldier, had fought hard all day. He had been shot in the shoulder but could not get medical assistance because his injury was light compared to so many others. In pain and too exhausted to do anything more, he bedded down on a corner of the battlefield. Nearby lay a Confederate soldier who was severely wounded. Feeling sorry for him, Aspinwall offered to share his blanket, and the soldier accepted. Though they had fought against each other hours before, now they lay under the stars and talked. The Confederate was growing weaker. Fearful he would die, he gave Aspinwall a card with the address and names of his wife and children and asked him to let his family know what had happened to him. Aspinwall promised he would. He drifted off to sleep, and when he awoke, the Confederate was dead.

Aspinwall couldn't write because of his shoulder injury, but he found another soldier who penned a letter to the Confederate's wife. Then he made his way to a Confederate field hospital and gave the letter to an officer, who thanked him and said he would see that it was delivered.

Such acts of kindness were not uncommon. Grant later wrote, "While a battle is raging one can see his enemy mowed down by the thousand, or the ten thousand, with great composure; but after the battle these scenes are distressing, and one is naturally disposed to do as much to alleviate the suffering of an enemy as a friend."

It had been a terrible day on both sides, with a combined estimate of over 8,000 men dead. In describing the Battle of Champion's Hill, one soldier commented, "We killed each other as fast as we could."

✴ ✴ ✴

ALL THAT NIGHT AFTER THE BATTLE, Pemberton's defeated soldiers retreated toward Vicksburg. When they got to the Big Black River bridge, twelve miles from the city, most of the army crossed on over. Because the hour was so late, the last 5,000 men, exhausted from their grueling day of battle, bedded down next to the river and slept behind a barricade of cotton bales. Many of them were injured, and all of them were demoralized. They were startled awake early the next morning to cries of alarm. As they pulled themselves to their feet, they learned that the Yankees had pursued them and were preparing to attack.

With their backs to the river, 5,000 Rebels faced 17,000 Federals. Suddenly, without waiting for anyone else, one of Grant's officers gave the signal for his division to advance, and 1,500 Yankee bluecoats, their bayonets ready, surged forward across a field and through the waist-high water of a bayou, then charged directly into the Confederate lines.

The mayhem lasted only three minutes. Overwhelmed, the retreating Rebels swarmed across the Big Black's bridge. Those who could not get to the bridge tried to swim the river, and many drowned. Another 1,700 were killed or captured before the Confederates could finally set fire to the bridge to stop the Yankee pursuit.

Fred was there and saw it all. When the Union troops charged the Confederate line, he recalled, "I became enthused with the spirit of the occasion, galloped across a cotton field, and went over the enemy's works with our men."

Fred was thrilled. The Confederates were in retreat. They were on the run! But at that very moment, as he savored this victory, his luck ran out. "Following the retreating Confederates to the Big Black, I was watching some of them swim the river," he recalled, "when a sharpshooter on the opposite bank fired at me and hit me in the leg."

With a cry of shock and pain, Fred fell to the ground. His leg was bleeding. Was this how his life would end? Bleeding to death on a battlefield? A moment later, one of Grant's aides "came dashing up and asked what was the matter. I promptly said, 'I am killed!' Perhaps because I was only a boy, the colonel presumed to doubt my word and said, 'Move your toes,' which I did with success.

"He then recommended our hasty retreat. This we accomplished in good order."

✷ ✷ ✷

PEMBERTON'S BEATEN ARMY struggled back to Vicksburg with less than half of the 22,000 soldiers that had set out days earlier to meet the Yankees. At the Big Black River, Grant and Sherman put part of their men to work constructing three temporary bridges to replace the bridge the Confederates had burned. Other soldiers foraged for food and looted homes in the area. Sherman stopped to drink water from a well near a log cabin and learned that the property belonged to Jefferson Davis. The house had been plundered by his troops, and Sherman found a book on the ground that was a copy of the United States Constitution. It would become a prized souvenir, for he noticed to his amazement that on the title page was written the name of the owner: Jefferson Davis, President of the Confederacy.

That night, when the bridges were complete, Grant's army began to move across the river. Sherman, an amateur artist, viewed the scene with a painter's eye. He wrote, "After dark, the whole scene was lit up with fires of pitch-pine. General Grant joined me there, as we sat on a log, looking at the passage of the troops by the lights of those fires; the bridge swayed to and fro under the passing feet, and made a fine war picture."

Fred's leg was attended to by a physician who removed the bullet and dressed the wound. Fred knew such an injury could be fatal if it became infected. The next day, he was still shaken from his experience and in pain from the wound, but he rode with his father and Sherman all the way to the bluffs north of Vicksburg. In the distance they could see the Mississippi River.

Grant felt Vicksburg was as good as taken. Very quickly he would silence the guns along the water, and the great Mississippi River would be completely in Federal hands. How could anyone doubt it? He had successfully transported his army south of Vicksburg. In the last eighteen days he had marched his men 200 miles into enemy territory and won five battles:

After Confederates burned the bridge over the Big Black River, Sherman's engineers constructed a pontoon bridge similar to this one on the James River in Virginia.

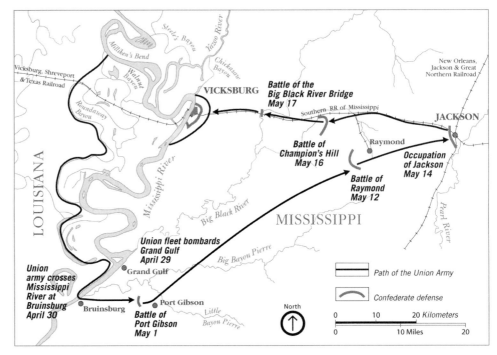

Grant's successes at Champion's Hill and the Big Black River put him in position to attack Vicksburg only eighteen days after getting his army onto Mississippi soil.

Grant's successes at Champion's Hill and the Big Black River put him in position to attack Vicksburg only eighteen days after getting his army onto Mississippi soil.

Grand Gulf, Port Gibson, Raymond, Champion's Hill, and the Big Black. He had defeated Pemberton, badly damaging and demoralizing the Rebel army.

As they gazed at the river on May 19, Sherman shook his head with amazement. He knew that what Grant had already accomplished would go down in military history as nothing short of brilliant.

"Until this moment," he said to his old friend, "I never thought your expedition a success. I never could see the end clearly until now."

ENEMY AT THE GATES

May 17–25, 1863

The weather in Vicksburg was sunny and clear the morning of Sunday, May 17. Mary Loughborough and a friend decided to go to church. They had not heard any news of Pemberton's army for several days and talked about this as they walked along. Near the Methodist church they met an officer they knew. He was visibly upset and told them the army had been twice defeated and that many citizens and all the town's doctors were headed out to care for the wounded. Mary was ready to turn around, but the church bells rang just then, beckoning her into the sanctuary. During the service, she worried about the men. Her husband had not marched out with Pemberton and was safe, but what did this news mean for Vicksburg?

Mary later wrote in her journal that as she and her friend walked home from church, they "passed groups of anxious men . . . In all the pleasant air and sunshine of the day [there was] a sorrowful waiting for tidings, that all knew now, would tell of disaster." Soon they saw the first retreating soldiers. The men, dirty and exhausted and some with bandages covering bloody wounds, kept their heads down as they trudged along. A few helped prop up injured comrades.

A woman standing near Mary and her friend asked the men, "Where on earth are you going?"

The embarrassed soldiers muttered, "We are running."

"Shame on you all!" another woman cried.

But quickly, sympathetic townspeople joined forces to feed them. Mary helped gather and prepare food. While the men ate, she listened to their stories of what had happened at Champion's Hill and the Big Black River. Some of the soldiers accused General Pemberton of selling them out to the Yankees because he was a Northerner. Mary observed, "Afterward we were told that General Pemberton behaved with courage—that the fault lay in the arrangement of troops . . . And where these weary and worn out men were going, we could not tell. I think they did not know themselves."

All that day and the next, retreating soldiers dragged into Vicksburg. Wagons and ambulances brought the wounded to the city's hospitals where townspeople joined the Sisters of Mercy in caring for them. Frightened refugees also poured in from the countryside to escape the Yankees— families with wagonloads of belongings, wealthy plantation owners riding in carriages, and poor folks on foot.

Pemberton faced a grave crisis. He was certain that Grant would lay siege to Vicksburg by surrounding the Confederate fortifications that ringed the little city, and that Union gunboats would not only attack from the river but also prevent any supplies from coming into the city by boat. How long could Pemberton's troops and the townspeople hold out? He knew his military history: a city under siege had to have help from the outside, or eventually it would starve. Pemberton had 32,000 soldiers and 5,000 townspeople—including 1,000 children—in his care. At most, current food supplies would last for a few weeks.

General Joe Johnston and his army needed to come to their rescue— and quickly.

In the meantime, Pemberton ordered his men to canvass the countryside around Vicksburg, confiscate any livestock and foodstuffs they could find on farms and plantations, and bring everything to the town's warehouses. From the porch of her elegant home, Emma Balfour watched the parade of people, animals, and goods coming into the city and wrote in her diary, "From twelve o'clock until late in the night the streets and roads were jammed with wagons, cannon, horses, men, mules, stock, sheep, everything you can imagine . . . being brought hurriedly within the entrenchment."

Emma was forty-four and the mother of six children. Her husband, William Balfour, was a prominent Vicksburg physician. Like other well-to-do families in Vicksburg, the Balfours had house slaves to attend to their needs and perform all household duties. The Balfour home high in the hills of Vicksburg had crystal chandeliers, a grand piano,

marble-topped tables, luxurious feather mattresses, and canopied beds. *Emma Balfour.* Emma was a noted hostess and often entertained. It was in the Balfour ballroom that the Christmas Eve Ball had been held.

Emma dreaded the idea of a siege, but she shared the conviction that Joe Johnston would save them. They would get along until he came. Right now they must help the bedraggled soldiers coming through the streets. That night she wrote, "I had everything that was eatable put out–

and fed as many as I could. Poor fellows, it made my heart ache to see them."

It was reassuring to know that Pemberton had left behind 10,000 soldiers to guard the city when he had gone out to meet Grant. They were rested and ready for combat, and as they marched through the streets, Mary Loughborough reported that chivalry—so much a part of the Southern code of honor—won the day as "the ladies waved their handkerchiefs, cheering them, and crying, 'These are the troops that have not run. You'll stand by us, and protect us, won't you? You won't retreat and bring the Federals behind you.' And the men, who were fresh and lively, swung their hats, and promised to die for the ladies—never to run—never to retreat."

The battle-weary soldiers from Champion's Hill and the Big Black River began to regroup and join the efforts to shore up defenses around the city. Soon everyone was working together, their spirits much improved. Still, Mary wrote, "What a sad evening we spent—continually hearing of friends and acquaintances left dead on the field, or mortally wounded and being brought in ambulances to the hospital. We almost feared to retire that night. No one seemed to know whether the Federal army was advancing. Some told us that they were many miles away, and others that they were quite near. How did we know but in the night we might be awakened by the tumult of their arrival!"

✻ ✻ ✻

PEMBERTON felt a surge of confidence when he inspected the eight miles of Confederate fortifications guarding Vicksburg. They were brilliant in concept. In some places, the trenches, rifle pits, and small forts were protected by deep ravines full of cane and underbrush, and in other places they were guarded by steep hills. In areas that were more open, the Confederates had cut down trees, dragged them in front of the trenches, and woven the branches together with wire and sharp stakes. To reach the trenches, the enemy had to get through this barricade first. The Confederates had only a hundred cannon, and to make it look like they had more, they had painted logs black and mounted them so they appeared to be regular cannon. These would help to fool the Yankees until Joe Johnston came to their rescue.

And he would come, wouldn't he? This worried Pemberton. Johnston's messages had stated that he felt Pemberton was going to have to surrender now that Grant had reached Vicksburg, and that trying to defend the city was a lost cause. But Pemberton and his generals were in agreement that they had to try. Their president, Jefferson Davis, wanted this, too. Pemberton continued asking Johnston for help. "I still conceive [Vicksburg] to be the most important point in the Confederacy," he wrote. And in one message he concluded, "I have decided to hold Vicksburg as long as possible."

✳ ✳ ✳

LIKE PEMBERTON, Ulysses Grant knew that Joe Johnston was the wild card. Up to now Johnston had avoided any actual confrontation with the Union army, but Grant knew from spies that he was only fifty miles away. Surely he must be getting reinforcements and would soon attack. Grant planned to take Vicksburg quickly, before that could happen. When he saw the hills and ravines and the impressive Confederate fortifications that protected the city's north, south, and east sides, he knew it wouldn't be easy. But Admiral Porter's naval fleet would fight from the river while Grant's troops attacked on land. There was no stopping his Army of the Tennessee. In the past twenty days Grant had achieved every goal, inflicting 7,000 casualties while losing only 4,500 of his own men. With reinforcements, he still had 31,000 troops. More reinforcements were on their way. Ammunition and supplies were plentiful. All the men were eager to finish this and to be the ones who opened the Mississippi River for the North.

Grant decided that the action would start at two o'clock sharp on May 19. It would begin with artillery fire, followed by the order to charge.

Vicksburg's powerful guns.

At that moment, thousands of bluecoats would rush forward, in some places forging through deep ravines, to scale the Confederate entrenchments, their guns blazing as they quickly overwhelmed the defenders. Grant expected little resistance and was so certain of victory that he had already directed his division commanders on how to keep their victorious soldiers under control when the battle was over.

Not everyone with Grant was as confident as he. A Union officer preparing to help storm the Confederate lines recorded what they were up against: "A long line of high, rugged, irregular bluffs clearly cut against the sky, crowned with cannon . . . Lines of heavy rifle pits . . . ran along the bluffs, connecting fort with fort, and [were] filled with veteran infantry. In front, on the slopes, was a tangle of fallen timber, tree-tops, interlaced to make an almost impenetrable abatis . . . The approaches to this position were frightful—enough to appall the stoutest heart."

A *New York Times* reporter who was with the Union troops was more succinct in his assessment, stating that the troops were now attempting to take a mountain.

✳ ✳ ✳

ON MAY 19, the bluecoats were in position. Precisely at two o'clock, commanders throughout the Union line gave the signal and artillery exploded in unison. The bluecoats charged, yelling at the tops of their lungs as they rushed forward. The Rebels were ready for them, and on signal from their own commanders, they fired straight into the Union line. Falling back, stumbling over the injured and dead, Grant's men tried again and again to storm the Confederate ridge, but each time they were driven back in an explosion of gunfire. Over and over, fresh troops moved forward to take the places of the men who fell.

Finally, with darkness coming on, Grant called a halt. The assault had failed. Almost a thousand of his men lay dead. One Union regimental flag had been shredded by fifty-five bullets.

Sherman said simply, "At every point we were repulsed." But to his wife he wrote, "This is a death struggle and will be terrible."

✳ ✳ ✳

THE REBELS WERE JUBILANT and the citizens of Vicksburg cheered in the streets. All afternoon Mary Loughborough and her friends had watched from Sky Parlor Hill and from the cupola of the courthouse. "The excitement was intense in the city," she wrote. "Groups of people stood on every available position where a view could be obtained of the distant hills, where the jets of white smoke constantly passed out from among the trees . . . The hills around near the city, and indeed every place that seemed commanding and secure, were covered with anxious spectators—many of them ladies—fearing the result of the afternoon's conflict."

That only 200 Confederate soldiers were killed seemed miraculous, though once again the wounded poured into the city's hospitals, where doctors, the dedicated Sisters of Mercy, and citizen volunteers cared for them.

Townspeople understood the significance of the day's victory for Pemberton and his troops. They became both hopeful and determined, their spirits renewed. But that night they had a taste of what would be required of them. Two Union gunboats moved into range and began to shell the city. They took occasional hits from the Vicksburg cannon on shore but were not damaged enough to stop firing.

"We ran to the small cave near the house," Mary said, "and were in it during the night . . . The caves were plainly becoming a necessity, as some persons had been killed on the street by fragments of shells . . . I shall never forget my extreme fear during the night, and my utter hopelessness of

Fred (shown here fourth from left) was liked and accepted by his father's officers. Grant (standing in the middle of the photo) is wearing a hat.

ever seeing the morning light. Terror stricken, we remained crouched in the cave, while shell after shell followed each in quick succession . . . Morning found us more dead than alive."

✻ ✻ ✻

GRANT TOOK TWO DAYS to rethink his strategy. In the meantime, he tightened the noose around Vicksburg: as of May 18 it was under siege. He also readied his men to try again. In spite of the pounding they had received, they had not lost their will to fight.

As Grant visited various points along the Union line, Fred rode beside him. He no longer desired to be in combat and spent part of each day resting in the tent he shared with his father. One of his worst fears had come true, for the wound in his leg had become infected. He had been with the army long enough to know he might lose his leg. He tried not to think of this possibility. He wanted to be an officer when he grew up—a military leader like his father. How could he do that with only one leg?

In spite of his own misery, he was still greatly interested in what was going on, and he listened while Grant and his officers laid out plans for their next assault on the Rebel fortifications. It would take place on May 22. All corps commanders would synchronize their timepieces and open fire in unison, at precisely ten o'clock in the morning.

On the appointed day, Union soldiers were realistic about what was ahead and tried to make certain that loved ones would receive their valuables in the event they were killed. One soldier wrote, "The boys were . . . busy divesting themselves of watches, rings, pictures, and other keepsakes, which were being placed in the custody of the cooks, who were not expected to go into action. I never saw such a scene before, nor do I want to see it again."

When the cannon sounded the attack, the men in blue rushed forward. One Union soldier tried to add some humor to his grim report of the assault: "We fixed bayonets and charged point blank for the rebel works at a double quick. Unfortunately for me I was in the front of the rank and compelled to maintain that position, and a glance at the forest of gleaming bayonets sweeping up from the rear, at a charge, made me realize that it only required a stumble of some lubber just behind me to launch his bayonet into the offside of my anatomy . . . This knowledge so stimulated me that I feared the front far less than the rear, and forged ahead like an antelope, easily changing my double quick to a quadruple gait . . . During that run and rush I had frequently to either step upon or jump over the bodies of our dead and wounded, which were scattered along our track."

Usually generals were positioned in safe places during battles, but in spite of the concern of his officers, Grant once again stayed with his men. Fred learned later that his father "had a narrow escape from a shell which was fired directly down a ravine which he had just entered. He was unhurt, but was covered with yellow dirt thrown up by the explosion."

Fred would never forget one particular incident. He was with his father and Sherman when a boy barely older than he "with blood streaming from a wound in his leg, came running up to where Father and Sherman stood, and reported that his regiment was out of ammunition. Sherman was directing some attention to be paid to his wound when the little fellow, finding himself fainting from loss of blood, gasped out, 'caliber 54,' as he was carried off to the rear. At this moment I observed that my father's eyes were filled with tears."

The young soldier was Orion Howe, a fourteen-year-old drummer boy from Illinois. His regiment was running low on .54-caliber ammunition, and he had volunteered to go for more. Union soldiers saw him running through heavy fire, determined to complete his errand. Most drummer boys like Orion Howe were very brave. Though they were sometimes as young as nine or ten, they played a critical role in battle, for their drumbeats relayed officers' orders. They had to stand where the most soldiers could hear them—sometimes in the open—and because they passed along such important information, they were targeted by enemy sharpshooters.

* * *

FINALLY GRANT HAD TO GIVE UP. His men were fighting heroically, but they were being mowed down and were accomplishing nothing. Grant called a halt. When it was all over, 3,200 Union soldiers were dead—more than had died in the five battles leading up to this day. The Confederates had fewer than 500 casualties. Grant realized he was not going to win Vicksburg either quickly or by storming the defenses. He would have to shell and starve Pemberton into submission. He would have to do it by siege.

That night, Union soldiers didn't dare try to rescue their wounded or dead lying close to Confederate lines. It was Pemberton who solved the problem. He proposed to Grant a truce for several hours so the Yankees could attend to these men and bury their dead.

Young Orion Howe with a Union officer.

Grant agreed, and during the truce on May 25, the soldiers from both sides met and mingled. A Union soldier wrote, "All the soldiers came out of their works and hiding places, and gave us a good opportunity to look at them. Many gibes and cuts were exchanged between the lines, in which the

Confederates seemed to hold their own." Another soldier reported that two Rebels and two Yankees played cards and swapped Southern tobacco for Northern coffee.

When the truce was over, the men wished each other good luck. Then they went back to their fortifications, aimed their rifles, and got back to the work of killing each other.

INTO THE CAVES

Late May and Early June 1863

As happy as Willie and his sisters were to be back in Vicksburg with their beloved father, the little city was a dangerous place. Dr. Lord impressed on his son that this was not a story from *Ivanhoe* or one of his other treasured adventure novels: the family was in real danger. Since May 18, Grant's army had formed a tight ring around Vicksburg, sealing it from the outside world. The city was under siege, and, as one soldier said, a cat could not slip out unnoticed.

Grant wanted the siege to end quickly, before Joe Johnston showed up. To hasten Vicksburg's surrender, he ordered his artillery units to shell it around the clock. The army aimed 220 cannon at military targets in the city and at the Confederate lines. Admiral Porter's navy aimed another thirteen big guns from the river. Shells flew fast and furious, sometimes crisscrossing in the air as they rained down death and destruction on the city and the Rebel soldiers. Cannonballs weighing as much as 250 pounds crashed through walls, tore up streets and yards, and exploded in the Confederate trenches. Highly skilled Union sharpshooters loaded their rifles with minié balls—powerful and precise bullets that could travel long distances and kill or maim in an instant. Thunderous explosions and the

This house, behind Union lines and badly damaged by shells, belonged to the Shirley family, who were Union sympathizers. Soldiers who camped in the yard created dugouts for shelter.

z-z-z-z-z-z-*pt* sound of these deadly bullets whizzing through the air terrorized both humans and animals. Like their elders, children quickly learned that their best chance of survival was to try to dodge minié balls. They should never try to outrun cannonballs, but stop and let them fly on over.

The Lord family soon found out that their home could not protect them. Willie's sister Lida reported that while the family was eating dinner, "a bombshell burst into the very center of the dining room, blowing out the roof and one side, crushing the well-spread table like an eggshell, and making a great yawning hole in the floor, into which disappeared our supper, china, and furniture."

Margaret Lord did not want to live in a cave, but after this incident her husband insisted. The family moved into a large communal cave that had been dug all the way through a hill. People could enter on one street

Townspeople tried to make their caves comfortable. Sometimes prayer helped ease worry and fear.

and exit onto another. Off the long hallway was a series of rooms, each with an outside entrance. Willie compared this layout to the prongs of a garden rake. He said there were many outside entrances so if "any one of them should collapse, escape could be made through the inner cave and its other branches." Entrances also gave fresh air, for the caves were otherwise hot and airless. Each of the rooms provided quarters for a family. The only privacy came from hanging blankets or setting up screens. Some house slaves slept in their family's quarters, while others slept near the entrances, as did soldiers recuperating from injuries. The rest of the hallway became a "commons." In this space, Willie said, "children played while their mothers sewed by candlelight or gossiped, and men fresh from trench or hospital gave news of the troubled outside world to spellbound listeners."

This cave, one of the largest in Vicksburg, was only one of an estimated 500 that dotted the city by the second week of the siege. There were so many caves that Union soldiers jokingly referred to the city as Prairie

Dog Town. Some caves were very small—just a dugout where people huddled for protection. Some had clusters of rooms and were elaborately decorated with carpets, mirrors, furniture, and beds. Townspeople brought their pillows and favorite quilts, musical instruments, china, and silver, and they hung pictures and built shelves to hold treasured photos, beloved books, and knickknacks or vases of flowers from their home gardens. Planks were laid on the ground to create flooring. Doorways were framed with wood, and walls were covered with rugs, pictures, or even wallpaper to give an illusion of cleanliness.

Outside, many people set up tents near cave entrances to shelter the cooking and eating area from sun and rain and to provide private places to dress. Because of the fire hazard, cooking had to be done in open air. During brief interludes each morning and evening when the shelling slowed or stopped, slaves labored over fires and cooking stoves to prepare meals for their masters. If they heard incoming shells, they ran into the caves.

As hard as people worked to make the caves comfortable, they were still dark and damp and home to lizards, mosquitoes, and other insects. Several days of heavy rains turned everything to mud. "It was living like plant roots," one woman reported. "We were in hourly dread of snakes. The vines and thickets were full of them, and a large rattlesnake was found one morning under a mattress on which some of us had slept all night."

At first Willie loved cave life, thinking of it as "the Arabian Nights made real. Ali Baba's forty thieves . . . lurked in the unexplored regions of the dimly lighted caves . . . and sent me off at night to fairyland on a magic rug." But he worried when his father left each morning to go to work "and we only knew him to be safe when he returned at night." He also grew tired of "squalling infants, family quarrels and the noise of general discord that were heard at intervals with equal distinctness." Not surprisingly, his mother had the hardest time. She implored her husband to have a cave dug for their private use. Dr. Lord gave in and agreed to see to it.

One of the other families living in this very large cave was Lucy's. Her father refused to leave the family home, even though, Lucy reported, "a

Minie ball passed through his whiskers as he sat in the hall, and lodged in the rocker of an old chair near him." Still, her mother couldn't budge him, so she had Rice and Mary Ann pack up necessities and she moved the rest of the family into the communal cave. Lucy thought there must have been about 200 people sharing this space, counting all the slaves and the recuperating soldiers. Class status disappeared. Poor whites slept next to wealthy plantation owners, and slaves slept next to their masters.

No one knew if they were actually safe. One night Lucy found out. She had stretched out on her bed—a wood plank covered with soft quilts—but couldn't get to sleep. She listened to the sounds around her. Outside, shells crashed and exploded. In a nearby room a young wife was in labor and would soon give birth. Finally Lucy got up and wandered into the main hallway. Several adults sat visiting by candlelight. One of them was Dr. Lord, who had a sore leg and foot. As Lucy later recalled, he was "all bandaged and propped on a chair for comfort. He said, 'Come here, Lucy, and lie down on this plank.' Dr. Lord was almost helpless, but he assisted me to arrange my bed, my head being just at his feet."

Lucy was finally drifting off to sleep when "suddenly a shell came down on the top of the hill, buried itself about six feet in the earth, and exploded. This caused a large mass of earth to slide . . . catching me under it. Dr. Lord, whose leg was caught and held by it, gave the alarm that a child was buried. Mother reached me first."

Lucy's frantic mother, assisted by Dr. Lord, "succeeded in getting my head out . . . [and] as soon as the men could get to me, they pulled me from under the mass of earth." Lucy was terrified, screaming and choking as she hemorrhaged blood from her mouth and nose. Her mother implored the physician attending the young wife in labor to examine Lucy, and he gave assurance that she had no broken bones "but he could not then tell what my internal injuries were."

At this very moment, a thunderous explosion shook the cave and Lucy watched as people became "frightened, rushing into the street screaming, and thinking that the cave was falling in. Just as they reached the street,

This photograph, taken after the war, shows an entrance to one of the caves. The cannonballs on display may have fallen nearby during the siege.

over came another shell bursting just above them, and they rushed into the cave again."

Unbelievably, Lucy reported, "during all this excitement there was a little baby boy born . . . He was called William Siege Green."

✳ ✳ ✳

WHEN ANOTHER SHELL STRUCK one of the cave entrances the next morning, Lucy's mother declared that she'd had enough. "Mother instantly decided to leave the cave," Lucy said, "and calling Rice and Mary Ann, she gathered clothing and bedding, determined to risk her life at home with Father. We left the cave about eight o'clock in the morning, having some distance to go to reach home. I was bent over from my injuries and could not run fast."

The little group finally reached its goal. "Father was horrified when he saw us," Lucy said, "and immediately made an effort to secure us another hiding place." Very quickly Mr. McRae located a cave closer to home and also deeper in the earth, making it safer. "A number of steps led down into this cave," Lucy remembered. "Mother had a tent pitched outside, so that when the mortars did not have the range we could sit there and watch the shells as they came over. They were beautiful at night."

Shortly after the McRaes left the communal cave, the Lord family experienced another fright there when one of the entrances suddenly collapsed. Willie wrote, "My father's powerful voice, audible above the roaring avalanche of earth as he shouted, 'All right! Nobody hurt,' quickly reassured us. But after these narrow escapes there was no longer a feeling of security even in the more deeply excavated portions of the cave."

Dr. Lord rushed the completion of the cave being dug for his family's private use by helping with the work. He had selected a location in a hill behind one of the hospitals, reasoning that "here, under the shadow of the yellow hospital flag which . . . was held sacred by all gunners in modern warfare, it was believed we should be comparatively safe." But eleven-year-old Willie quickly realized that shells were falling everywhere, including on the hospital. Another Vicksburg hospital took a direct hit from a shell, killing eight and wounding fourteen. A surgeon buried under the rubble saved himself from bleeding to death by tying off an artery. His leg was later amputated. In spite of the constant danger, the women of Vicksburg continued to volunteer in the hospitals.

Willie's mother and youngest sister had a very close call one day when two large shells fell nearby and exploded simultaneously, filling the air with flames and smoke. Willie's mother tried to soothe her four-year-old daughter, saying, "Don't cry, my darling. God will protect us." To which the girl replied that she was afraid that God had already been killed.

In spite of the danger, Margaret Lord was much happier in this private cave, which was shaped like the letter L and had two entrances, allowing some circulation of air inside. She wrote, "In this cave we sleep and live literally under ground. I have a little closet dug for provisions, and niches for flowers, lights and books. Just by the little walk is our eating table with an arbor over it, and back of that our fireplace and kitchen with table . . . This is quite picturesque and attractive to look at but Oh! How wearisome to live!"

Her children, she said, "bear themselves like little heroes." Her husband also did his part. Every day Dr. Lord opened Christ Episcopal Church and, according to Willie, he "rang the bell, robed himself in priestly garb, and . . . with the deep boom of cannon taking the place of organ notes and the shells of the besieging fleet bursting around the sacred edifice, he preached the gospel of eternal peace."

With his ability to calm, Dr. Lord served as comfort to the townspeople and soldiers who risked shells and bullets to attend his services. During the first few weeks of the siege, Emma Balfour often attended Dr. Lord's services and noted in her diary, "The church has been considerably damaged and was so filled with bricks, mortar and glass that it was difficult to find a place to sit." The Catholic church continued to host daily mass. The few churches that remained open usually had people sleeping in their pews at night because they felt safer there than in caves.

✹ ✹ ✹

EMMA BALFOUR STILL REFUSED to move her household into a cave. She took shelter in one when the shelling was heavy, but she always felt like she was suffocating when she was underground. At home, she kept an eye on the river, concerned that the Federals would launch an all-out attack. Sometimes she and a friend or two would brave the shelling and go to Sky Parlor Hill for a better view. Ten days into the siege, she had seen the sinking of a Union gunboat, the *Cincinnati*, considered one of the finest in the Union fleet, when it was hit by the Vicksburg waterfront cannon. "We are again victorious on water!" she had declared. A Confederate soldier said that hundreds of women watched from Sky Parlor Hill. "There were loud cheers, the waving of handkerchiefs, amid general exultation, as the vessel went down," he said.

As the siege wore on, some Union soldiers expressed concern for the townspeople. They did not take lightly to starving and shelling old people, women, and children. One soldier said, "I can't pity the rebels themselves but it does seem too bad for the women and children in the city." Another wrote, "I suppose [the women] are determined to brave it out. Their sacrifices and privations are worthy of a better cause, and were they but on our side, how we would worship them."

Emma surmised why the Federals bombarded Vicksburg so ruthlessly. "The general impression is that they fire at this city, in that way thinking that they will wear out the women and children and sick, and General Pemberton will be impatient to surrender the place on that account, but they little know the spirit of the Vicksburg women and children if they expect this.

"Rather than let them know that they are causing us any suffering, I would be content to suffer martyrdom!"

DANGEROUS DAYS

Early June 1863

For the people inside the besieged city, each new day brought only one goal: survival. Emma Balfour wrote in her diary, "After passing a bad night from the bursting of bombs around us, we were roused this morning by the whistling of parrott shells and I assure you we dressed hurriedly. They came so thick and fast that it seemed a miracle that none came in the windows or against the house." Another day she wrote, "The most fearful cannonading commenced from the lines. I never saw anything like it. People were running in every direction to find a place of safety. The shells fell literally like hail."

Like other Vicksburg residents, the Balfours cared for sick and injured soldiers. Almost every home became a hospital. Tents were put up alongside the actual hospitals to house even more patients. Mary Loughborough sent what food she could to recuperating soldiers. She had close calls of her own. During one heavy bombardment, a huge shell landed just outside her cave, "rocking the earth, followed by a deafening explosion, such as I had never heard before. The cave filled instantly with powder, smoke and dust. I stood with a tingling, prickling sensation in my head, hands and feet, and with a confused brain. Yet alive! Child, servants, all here, and saved!"

When a live shell rolled into the cave, only the quick action of one of the slaves, who picked it up and threw it outside, kept them from being killed. After that, Mary's husband found her a new cave very near the front lines. Ironically, there was less danger there than in the city, where there had already been many injuries and several deaths. Mary felt the weight of all this. "How very sad this life in Vicksburg! How little security can we feel," she wrote, "with so many around us seeing the morning light that will never more see the night!"

Along with other children living in the caves, Lucy had to learn to make the best of her situation. But the close calls were always frightening, especially in the caves. She experienced several incidents when "the shot fell thick and fast. We sat, or stood, under the ground, looking at one another in speechless fear . . . thinking that each moment would be our last. When we could look out upon the daylight it was with thankful hearts that we had been spared through that battle." During lulls in the shelling, she and her brothers entertained themselves by playing cards, making up games, and reading books. Some children collected spent shells, cartridges, and minié balls. School had been disrupted by all the troubles, but during the long days in the caves, some children kept up their lessons.

Out and about in the city each day, Dr. Lord had several close calls. He knew to stand perfectly still when he heard an incoming shell and let it go on over him. But one day he was with an acquaintance when they both heard that distinct sound. According to Willie, in spite of his father's warn-

This painting by the noted artist Howard Pyle shows the danger when shells fell on Vicksburg.

ings, the other man began to run. He had made it only a few yards, "when the shell exploded directly in his path, leaving him a mangled corpse by the roadside, while my father stood unharmed."

Dr. Lord also witnessed a highly unusual accident. As Willie related, "The victim . . . stood holding an officer's horse . . . [when a] ball struck [his] head from his shoulders and left the headless trunk, still holding the reins of the horse and standing as erect and soldier-like as when alive. The noiseless cannonball had so quietly done its deadly work that the horse took no alarm, but stood as still as the corpse that held it. In a moment the men on the street rushed to the spot, and the horse then reared in fright and the body fell to the pavement. To my father it seemed an almost interminable length of time that the dead soldier held the living horse, whereas in reality it was a matter of a few seconds." Willie said his father would never forget the horror of that incident.

A small girl was struck by a bullet but was not seriously injured. A physician removed the bullet and, according to Willie, a clever soldier recovering in the hospital carved it into a miniature set of knives and forks, "to the girl's infinite pride and delight."

Willie himself suffered a close call. He bent to pick up something and at that very moment a minié ball flew past him, "so near the top of my head as to stir my hair." Willie never forgot "that I had narrowly escaped death." He kept the unexploded shell as a souvenir.

And Lucy was almost killed when she and her mother were in the tent outside their cave entrance. Her mother was brushing Lucy's hair when they heard a shell coming toward them. "Get in the cave!" Lucy's mother cried. Lucy recalled, "She did get in, but I had only time to jump into a small hole we children had dug out in the side of the hill when a piece of the shell came down into the tent, demolishing the washstand by which we had stood. I felt the heat as it came down. Mother's face, white with anxiety for me, peeped out from the cave door. There I sat, stunned with fear."

One day an officer told Mrs. McRae that firing would be heavy around their cave and he thought they would be safer near the front lines under cover of the hills. Lucy's mother decided they should go. "So," reported Lucy, "up came the tent, a large basket was quickly packed with the meager stock of provisions, and away we went across Glass Bayou Bridge, climbing the hill on the other side of the bridge late in the evening, and traveling the road just behind our batteries, where all along were dug trenches for our soldiers to fight behind. This was a very dangerous route by daylight, but under cover of night we felt safe."

They pitched their tent near other residents also seeking safety and went to sleep. Just before daylight they were awakened by the thunderous boom of cannon "and before we could think where we were, a cannonball that had spent its force on the side of the hill came rolling into the tent . . . and in less time than it takes to tell it we were all up and out of the tent. Balls were whizzing, cannon booming from the rear, mortars replying in rapid succession from the front."

Lucy's mother called out orders. "Rice! Take that tent up and let us go to town!" Rice replied, "Yes, Ma'am," and set to work "while the shot were falling around. An officer whom Mother knew rushed up and cried, 'Mrs. McRae, keep close under the bank, and don't take the road until you are obliged to.' He afterward said he never expected us to reach town."

Lucy would never forget that treacherous journey to reach safety and the fear that stalked every moment of it. "On we came," she remembered, "jumping behind trees, fences, or into trenches, shells exploding above us, scattering their pieces around us. We children were crying, Mother praying, all running between the shells . . . trying to reach Glass Bayou Bridge . . . Rice had dropped the tent and Mary Ann the lunch basket, and as we came to the bridge a mortar shell exploded at the other end. We all fell to the ground, and when we got to our feet again not a word was spoken except 'Run!' and we did run. Mother had me by the hand pulling me, while my brothers were close by us."

Finally reaching safety, they collapsed, both exhausted and thankful.

✻ ✻ ✻

As THE SIEGE WORE ON, food supplies dwindled. There was still water in the city's cisterns, but only enough for cooking and drinking, with none to spare for bathing or washing clothes. Residents went weeks without changing clothes, their skin grimy with the dirt from the caves and the residue from all the explosions. At night they huddled in darkness underground, stuffed together, sweltering from the heat and humidity, enduring mosquitoes, ticks, chiggers, and other biting insects, fearful of snakes and lizards, suffering temporary deafness from the thunderous explosions, their nerves frayed from fear. Each day houses and businesses burned or were pounded into rubble. Deep craters created by the shelling dotted the landscape. Hospitals overflowed, and those who could do so assisted the Sisters of Mercy in nursing patients.

Yet in spite of how bad the situation was becoming, when several citizens started a petition to get Pemberton to ask Grant for a truce so women and children could leave the city, only those few who proposed it would sign it. Others felt strongly that this was their city and this was their cause and they were in this fight to the finish.

Every day, everyone looked hopefully to the east, straining to hear the sounds of Joe Johnston coming to their rescue. Though persistent rumors said he would appear any moment leading 100,000 Rebel troops ready to fight, try as they might, nobody in Vicksburg could hear anything.

GROWING DESPERATION

Mid June 1863

Ulysses Grant knew those Joe Johnston rumors and he took them seriously. With the arrival of reinforcements, he now had 77,000 troops under his command—over twice Pemberton's numbers. Grant needed every man. He had to be prepared for the possibility of a two-sided fight: Pemberton on one side of him and Joe Johnston on the other. But as June wore on, he wondered if Johnston would ever get there.

So did Pemberton. The Union kept cutting the telegraph lines, and it could take couriers as long as two weeks to deliver messages from one general to the other, for to avoid capture they had to stay off main roads and travel through woods and swamps. In his messages to Johnston, Pemberton voiced both confidence and desperation. Johnston told him to hold on, that help was coming. Pemberton asked, "When shall I expect you?" Another time he wrote, "I am waiting most anxiously to know your intentions . . . I shall endeavor to hold out as long as we have anything to eat."

Rumors to the contrary, Johnston had only 32,000 men in his Army of Relief. Still, that was enough when combined with Pemberton's 30,000 to take on Grant. But Johnston wasn't moving. He had received a serious wound in battle months earlier, and some speculated that he was still recov-

A West Point graduate, Joe Johnston was often at odds with Jefferson Davis. He was defeated or contributed to losses at Vicksburg, Stones River, Chickamauga, Chattanooga, and Atlanta.

ering, while others wondered if he had lost his will to fight. Jefferson Davis urged him to go to Vicksburg's aid, but Johnston replied that he did not have enough men and thought saving Vicksburg was hopeless. So he did nothing.

While this stalemate in Confederate leadership continued, both the Yankees and the Rebels persisted in their daily standoff in the trenches at Vicksburg. Every day General Grant rode along the twelve miles of front lines. He dressed like a private so Rebel sharpshooters wouldn't recognize him as he visited various state regiments. Fred was usually with his father, even though he wasn't feeling well. "The wound I had received early in the campaign now began to trouble me very much," he said, "and, under Dr. Hewitt's expressed fears of having to amputate my leg, I remained much at headquarters."

Few medicines existed to help fight infections like Fred's. Penicillin had not yet been discovered, and soldiers who did not bleed to death from their wounds often died from such infections, particularly if they were wounded in the stomach or chest. Doctors could amputate wounded arms or legs to prevent infection or to keep it from spreading—though the amputation site itself could also become infected and prove fatal.

Instead of spending his time with the soldiers, Fred wanted to be near his father. As a result, he said, "I saw a great deal of my father's methods, his marvelous attention to detail, and his cool self-possession. I also witnessed the devotion of his men to him, and the enthusiasm with which they greeted . . . him, when he passed along the line. Father was a splendid horseman, and visited many points of his army every day."

A volunteer health inspector who was visiting the camp remembered Fred, who had turned thirteen in May, on his daily rounds with his father: "Almost every day as I drove about the lines, at some point or other I would see General Grant and his brave little assistant, riding at full speed in the face of the long lines of the enemy's batteries, and within range of their murderous fire.

"Fred Grant shared his father's dangers; and although he was one of the nicest boys I ever saw, few knew his real merits and bravery. Like his distinguished father, he was free from bombast and was quiet and reserved, so his heroic services during the siege were not paraded before the public . . . It was fortunate that his devoted mother was not there at that time to see his danger as he went out under the guns daily. Her anxiety would have been unbearable."

Julia Grant would also have been concerned about her son's health, for Fred was now suffering from typhoid fever and dysentery as well as the infection in his leg. Grant finally became alarmed enough that he sent Fred to Kentucky to recuperate with Julia Grant's sister, Emma Casey. Bands of Confederate guerrillas roamed the Kentucky countryside, and a week after Fred arrived, a man dressed like a Confederate officer came into Emma Casey's yard on his horse and asked for a drink of water.

She later wrote, "He said casually, 'I guess Fred Grant is visiting you, isn't he?' Instantly a cold suspicion struck me like a dart through the heart and I answered him as casually as he had questioned me, 'Why, no.'

" 'Oh,' he said. 'Isn't he?'

" 'No, he's gone.'

" 'Gone, has he? Is that so?' "

The man left and Fred's badly frightened aunt immediately put him on a boat back to Vicksburg, certain he was safer there. Emma Casey said that later that day, eight "hard-riding, grim-looking, and tattered cavalrymen rode up to the gate. One of them, heavily armed, and looking as fierce as a

Greek bandit, came up to the porch." The man asked if a boy was visiting there and Emma said that a boy had been there but was now gone. When the man questioned whether she was sure, she said she was and that some Union gunboats would be coming up the river shortly. "Perhaps you gentlemen will be interested in seeing them," she said bravely. The men laughed, wished her a good day, and rode away. Emma later worried about what impact Fred's capture might have had on the Union cause. Fortunately, Fred reached his father safely. When he arrived, Grant wrote to his wife that their son did not look very well but insisted on staying until Vicksburg fell.

So Fred stayed, and he did not lose his confidence that Vicksburg would soon surrender. He was still determined to be there on that great day.

✴ ✴ ✴

GRANT HAD SELECTED SHERMAN to take charge of the eastern front. During the long days of the siege, while he and his army watched and waited for Joe Johnston, Sherman sometimes took breaks by riding his horse through the countryside. One day he stopped at a nearby plantation where a number of Southern families had sought refuge. He learned that one of them was the Wilkinson family of New Orleans and asked if their son had been a cadet at Alexandria, Louisiana, when he was superintendent of the military academy there. Mrs. Wilkinson confirmed this and said her son was now fighting for the South at Vicksburg.

Sherman wrote, "I then asked about her husband, whom I had known, when she burst into tears, and cried out in agony, 'You killed him at Bull Run, where he was fighting for his country!' I disclaimed killing anybody at Bull Run; but all the women present (nearly a dozen) burst into loud lamentations, which made it most uncomfortable for me, and I rode away."

Ordinary soldiers couldn't go on country rides, but they still found

ways to take breaks. Pemberton's men had to stay in the trenches, but the Yankees got time off and played cards, sang, wrote letters to the folks back home or wrote in their journals (provided they could write), cleaned their guns, played baseball, whittled on pieces of wood, swapped stories with tent mates, and carried on camp life. Books were treasured, and at night around a campfire, men who were literate sometimes read aloud to an eager audience. The novels of Charles Dickens were especially popular. The 8th Wisconsin Infantry had a distraction in their pet eagle, nicknamed Old Abe in honor of the president. The young eagle traveled with the men on his own perch. Stories—which may or may not be true—abounded that he also went into battle with them, screeching loudly as he flew above the heads of the enemy.

Life under the broiling Mississippi sun proved difficult for both sides. Southerners, who were used to the heat and humidity, had some advantage. They also knew how to co-exist with native creatures—unlike one Yankee from Michigan who almost lost his life when he went swimming in the

A game of cards was a popular way to pass time when soldiers weren't on duty.

*The 8th
Wisconsin
Infantry's pet
eagle, Old Abe,
on his perch.*

Yazoo River and was attacked by an alligator. Rats infested the trenches, and mosquitoes, flies, chiggers, fleas, lice, and lizards bedeviled everybody, especially at night. Officers lucky enough to sleep on cots set the cot legs in jars of water, which kept lizards from climbing into their beds.

Believing that perspiration was good for the body, nobody questioned soldiers' wearing wool uniforms, even though they added to the men's misery. The camps stank. Sanitation, always a problem for an army, was made worse by the oppressive heat. Anyone approaching either army could smell it before they saw it. Horses and mules compounded the problem. Soldiers on both sides suffered all kinds of health maladies. Epidemics of measles and mumps broke out. Malaria, tuberculosis, typhoid fever, and smallpox killed many. Some water sources became contaminated from dead animals, causing yet more sickness.

When the men were in the trenches, they had to stay alert every moment against sudden attack and to keep their heads down so they wouldn't be spotted by enemy sharpshooters. Sometimes, as a diversion, a soldier would put a hat on a stick and hold it up for the sport of seeing how many enemy bullets would be fired at it. Or soldiers attached mirrors to poles and held them up so they could see into the other side's trenches, which in some places were only a few yards away.

At night when officers weren't around, the Rebels and Yanks occasionally visited back and forth or even left their trenches to talk, joke, taunt each other, and share photos of loved ones. A Union soldier later wrote of one of these meetings, "From the remarks of some of the Rebels, I judged that their supply of provisions was getting low, and that they had no source from which to draw more. We gave them from our own rations some fat meat, crackers, coffee, and so forth."

One day a private from Wisconsin simply said to the Yanks around

Where hillsides allowed it, the Union army sometimes carried out its work on two levels, with soldiers topside doing the fighting, while soldiers below rested or attended to other duties.

him that he was going to shake hands with the Rebs. He set down his gun and climbed out of his trench. Before long, several hundred men from both sides were out in the open exchanging news and trading Southern tobacco for Northern coffee. When a Union officer broke up the party, the men returned to their trenches and resumed shooting at each other.

Said one soldier of the enemy, "They agreed with us perfectly on one thing: If the settlement of this war was left to the enlisted men of both sides, we would soon go home."

EMPTY STOMACHS

Late June 1863

n the North, pressure mounted on Grant to finish the job. Vicksburg had been under siege for five long weeks—since May 18—and still had not surrendered. Trench warfare could go on endlessly. Grant and his army were needed to fight in other places, especially now, when Robert E. Lee, the Confederacy's most powerful general, was invading the North.

Grant pushed harder. He had his men dig a tunnel under the Rebel lines and pack it with explosives. The blast that followed created a huge crater that allowed the Federals to rush through the tunnel, climb up and out of the crater, and emerge behind enemy lines. They thought they would quickly overpower their stunned opponents. Instead, the Rebels had heard the digging, guessed what the Yanks were up to—and were waiting for them. Bloody hand-to-hand combat ensued, until the Federals had to retreat. They lost 200 men and the Confederates lost 100.

Grant didn't give up on tunnel warfare. He put his men to work digging more tunnels. He continued around-the-clock shelling of the Confederate lines and the city. Something would have to make these Southerners give up! Maybe it would finally be starvation. They couldn't hold out forever—and it sure didn't look like Joe Johnston planned to do anything about it.

Thirty-five Union soldiers who had been coal miners before the war dug a forty-five-foot-long tunnel under Rebel entrenchments. The explosion of 2,200 pounds of gunpowder in the tunnel created a crater that gave Union forces access behind enemy lines.

✳ ✳ ✳

INSIDE VICKSBURG, townspeople worried about the suffering of the soldiers in the trenches but could barely take care of themselves. Night and day shells fell, exploding into a thousand dangerous fragments. Because people stayed in the caves, there were few deaths, but Willie said that "all lived in a state of terror."

A woman who was busy cooking when a shell exploded nearby grabbed a hot pot off her stove and ran through the streets to her cave, not even aware that she was still holding the pot. Lucy reported that "one lady standing in a cave door had her arm taken off" by a minié ball whizzing by. When the writer Mark Twain later interviewed Vicksburg residents about this time, one told him, "Sometimes a cave had twenty or twenty-five people packed into it; no turning room for anybody; air so foul, sometimes, you couldn't have made a candle burn in it."

✳ ✳ ✳

AN INCIDENT OCCURRED on a narrow footpath up a steep hill from the Lord cave that revealed how slaves often regarded whites. According to Willie, a young black boy was guiding a white nun along the footpath from the hospital where she had assisted wounded soldiers. They met a Confederate corporal who saluted the Sister and stepped aside so she could pass, but, Willie wrote, "as she was about to do so a shell of the smaller kind, with a slowly burning fuse, fell in the pathway at his feet." Realizing the danger, the soldier tumbled backward down the hill to safety. At that moment, "the black hero," as Willie referred to the boy, grabbed the shell and pitched it away.

" 'Why did you not do that at once?' asked the trembling Sister. 'The moment you waited might have cost us all our lives.' "

The slave child carefully replied that he had "too much respect" for white folks to do a thing like that while the "gentleman" was standing there—meaning he didn't dare reach in front of a white man to do what the white man should have done, for a slave could be whipped or sold for such an infraction.

A white soldier at Milliken's Bend reported that the Union's untested black recruits fought like tigers.

But slavery was coming to an end. Unless they lived on isolated plantations, blacks in the South during the Civil War knew about Abraham Lincoln's Emancipation Proclamation, issued in January 1863, giving freedom to slaves in states under Union control. Grant had 10,000 to 12,000 newly liberated slaves with his army at Vicksburg.

Blacks must have been jubilant to hear that former slaves who had joined the Union army had fought bravely in a battle against Confederate troops on June 7 at Milliken's Bend, not far from Vicksburg. Though the black regiment had suffered heavy casualties, the men had held their own and beaten back their attackers. This event had changed the minds of many who felt blacks did not have the ability to fight. Frederick Douglass, the famous black abolitionist, had pleaded, "Give them a chance. I don't say that they will fight better than other men. All I say is, give them a chance!" When they got the chance and proved their mettle, a Southern senator commented, "If slaves seem good soldiers, then our whole theory of slavery is wrong."

Assistant Secretary of War Charles Dana wrote, "The bravery of the blacks in the battle at Milliken's Bend completely revolutionized the sentiment of the military." Indeed, starting that summer of 1863, blacks were

Black soldiers, who quickly proved their worth and willingness to fight, were commanded by white officers, many of whom died in combat alongside their men.

increasingly recruited into the Union army, with nearly 200,000 eventually fighting for the North. Toward the end of the war, the South, which had some black soldiers all along, would recruit them as well.

But for now, in Vicksburg, many blacks were with their white masters in the caves, simply hoping to survive the siege. As much as he wanted his freedom, Rice remained loyal to Lucy's family. Their fate was his fate. At night, when Lucy covered her ears and tried to bury her head in her pillow so she couldn't hear the exploding shells, Rice was there, too.

✳ ✳ ✳

ONCE A PROUD and beautiful community of grand homes and splendid gardens, Vicksburg was almost in ruins. Anyone pausing long enough to study the buildings around them saw that every glass pane in every house and building had shattered. Many windows had been boarded up.

Townspeople held on. Both Willie and Lucy read the one-sheet newspaper that was issued daily, though it had to be printed on the back of wallpaper once all the regular paper had been used up. It always offered assurance that "Old Joe" was going to come to the rescue and that together he and General Pemberton would defeat General Grant.

✳ ✳ ✳

BY THE END OF JUNE, dwindling supplies of food and water grew critical. The city's wells were almost dry, and drinking water was rationed to only one cup of water per day per person. Confederate soldiers dipped water out of mud holes and sometimes resorted to drinking dirty river water. A few residents had their own wells, and some of them sold water—Margaret Lord had to buy it for her family, paying for it by the bucket. Others with wells freely gave away the water until it was gone. It was the same with food: some who had it sold it on the black market for

FRONT: WALLPAPER   BACK: NEWSPAPER

After reading the newspaper printed on the back of wallpaper, some residents hung the patterned side on the walls of their caves as decoration.

high prices, while others gave it to whoever needed it—proving, as always, that hard times could bring out the best, as well as the worst, in people.

After all the chickens, cows, horses, and mules had been used for food, dogs and cats and other family pets began to disappear. Soon there were no birds or squirrels to be seen. Mary Loughborough finally consented to her little daughter's pet bird being made into soup for the child, who was ill and needed nourishment.

Lucy said of her family's situation, "Our provisions were becoming scarce, and the Louisiana soldiers were eating rats as a delicacy . . . Mother would not eat mule meat, but we children ate some, and it tasted right good, having been cooked nicely. Wheat bread was a rarity, and sweetpotato coffee was relished by the adults." Indeed, there were several variations on "Confederate coffee," including concoctions made of corn, okra, or even rye flour, if it could be had.

The specter of hunger haunted both soldiers and civilians. Everyone's stomach rumbled. Willie reported that his family was down to "a halfbarrel of [corn] meal and about the same quantity of sugar, so that like everyone else, we began to look forward with anxiety to what might await us in the near future."

Poor people in Vicksburg had even less to eat than the soldiers, and the threat of starvation was very real for them. Hardest hit were impoverished mothers whose husbands were at war or had died and who had hungry children to feed. They searched for tree buds, weeds, and cane shoots, mixing them with blackberries and half-ripe peaches to make a sort of stew. They pulled up the flooring in smokehouses in search of crystals of salt. Soldiers raided gardens, and townspeople, both rich and poor, had to guard what few vegetables they still had.

Soldiers' daily rations were cut, and then cut again, shrinking to a couple of biscuits, a little bacon, and a handful of rice. By the end of June, army rations had been reduced to 14.5 ounces of food per day—just a little rice, and pea bread.

Pea bread. No one who survived the siege of Vicksburg would ever forget it. The one food item still plentiful, for some reason, was peas, and army cooks learned to make bread from pea meal. "It was awful," one soldier recalled, "either rubbery or hard as rock, and in either case foul-tasting." Another said it was like leather to digest. Townspeople and patients in the hospital also ate the terrible bread when there was nothing else to eat, and some got sick from it.

Even as the situation grew more desperate, few people talked about surrender. They still believed in Joe Johnston. Humor helped. A citizen distributed cards for the fictitious "Hotel de Vicksburg," featuring a menu of Mule Tail Soup, Pea Meal Pudding, and Genuine Confederate Coffee.

Soldiers also managed an occasional laugh. Confederate pickets asked their Union counterparts one night what they had to eat. The Northerners, who had ample supplies, gave a long list: good coffee, beef, bread, and so forth. They then asked what the Southerners had, knowing that they were starving. But the Southerners replied with what could only have been a wish list, stating that they had butter and cake and biscuits, among other tasty items—to which a Yank added for them, "and pea meal." The Southerner who told this story said, "Then we all roared."

Though some Confederates deserted, going over to the Federals so they would be fed, most held fast. A Southern general said of his men, "I have rarely heard a murmur of complaint. The tone has always been, 'This is pretty hard, but we can stand it.'"

But they could not do so forever.

By the first day of July, forty-five days into the siege, the men were so weak that General Pemberton feared they didn't have the strength to withstand an all-out attack from the Federals, or to try to break out from their lines—even if Old Joe did arrive to help. Half the men were on the sick list or in the hospital. Many had swollen ankles, a symptom of scurvy, which was caused by vitamin deficiency. So many soldiers died that coffin builders could not keep up, and the dead were buried in trenches, covered by blankets. An officer wrote, "Graves are dug today for use tomorrow."

Union troops continued digging tunnels, thirteen in all, and filled them with explosives. They would all be set off on July 6, the day that Grant planned a major attack on Confederate forces. It was time to end this.

General Sherman, still guarding the eastern front, was certain that any attempt to take Vicksburg would come with a price. One thing he knew by now was that Southerners, weak or not, would fight to the finish. He told his wife in a letter that he needed all his cunning and all his strength, for these Rebels, he said, fight like devils.

SURRENDER!

July 4, 1863

Responding to Confederate pressure to try to save Vicksburg, Joe Johnston finally set out for the city on July 1. But by the time General Pemberton received his message to expect him on July 7, it was already too late.

✳ ✳ ✳

PEMBERTON KNEW IT WAS THE END. He had received an anonymous letter, probably from his own troops (though this was never determined), that was signed "Many Soldiers," telling him, "If you can't feed us, you had better surrender us." On July 2 he called his generals together to decide what to do. Their meager rations would run out in a few days. Doctors treating the sick and wounded had no more medicine. Because so many men were ill or injured, the 19,000 soldiers still in the trenches had to stay there all day and night, with no relief. They were too weak to fight well, and if the North launched an all-out attack, it would surely be a bloodbath. The generals also knew how much the townspeople were suffering.

Nobody wanted to give up. But was it right to continue in the face of

At Champion's Hill, General John Bowen led a counterattack that almost defeated the Federals.

such overwhelming odds? Was it fair to sacrifice more lives to a cause that now seemed hopeless?

Pemberton was painfully aware that he would be blamed for the loss of Vicksburg. The only way to salvage his reputation was to lead his soldiers in an attempt to break through the Union lines and unite with Johnston's army to fight Grant and Sherman. "This is my only hope of saving myself from shame and disgrace," he told his generals. But when they voted to surrender, Pemberton nodded in agreement, feeling he must "sacrifice myself to save the army which has so nobly done its duty to defend Vicksburg." He said he would officially surrender the city on the Fourth of July.

Startled, his generals protested that doing so on America's greatest holiday would be too humiliating for Southerners. Pemberton reminded them that he was a Northerner and knew the North's "national vanity." He said, "I know we can get better terms from them on the Fourth of July than on any other day of the year. We must sacrifice our pride to these considerations."

In what must have been one of the hardest things he had ever done, Pemberton wrote to Grant, requesting that they meet to discuss Vicksburg's surrender. He chose General John Bowen, who had fought valiantly at Champion's Hill, to deliver this message. Bowen was thirty-two and prior to the war had been an architect in St. Louis, where he and Grant had been friends and neighbors. Bowen hoped their friendship might help in negotiating the terms of surrender.

Bowen was so ill with dysentery that to even get on his horse required all his strength. But the next morning, July 3, with an aide riding next to him holding a flag of truce, the young officer rode toward the Union lines. Soldiers saw the white flag and held their fire. For the first time in forty-seven days, the air was silent. Men in the trenches on both sides climbed out, met in the middle, and talked in hushed tones. Was this merely a break to bury the dead?

Or was it something else?

Riding slowly, the day's heat and humidity already at suffocating intensity, Bowen reached Union headquarters and handed over Pemberton's note. He asked to speak to Grant but was informed that the general would not see him, for he was not willing to discuss terms for the surrender. Grant held all the cards: Confederate deserters had confirmed that the Rebels were weak from starvation and could not hold out long. Grant's all-out assault on July 6 would finish them off. But while Grant's note back to Pemberton stated that he would only accept an unconditional surrender, he added that he would be willing to meet with Pemberton at three o'clock that afternoon.

This was something, at least, and Bowen rode back to deliver Grant's message. Then, pale with pain, he turned around and headed back once again to the Union lines to announce Pemberton's agreement. Shortly before three that afternoon, Bowen was by Pemberton's side, along with one other officer, as they rode to a spot between the two camps to meet Grant. Men in gray and blue watched in silence. Pemberton was determined to get some concessions for his men. An unconditional surrender would send them all to Northern prison camps—and those vile places, so full of disease, were a death sentence just as surely as was remaining in the trenches at Vicksburg.

In the Union camp, thirteen-year-old Fred was so excited about the afternoon's meeting that he could almost forget how sick he was. Though already miserable because of his leg wound and typhoid fever, Fred's dysentery had gotten worse. "Dysentery had pulled me down from 110 pounds to sixty-eight pounds and I had a toothache as well," Fred remembered. Sick or not, he wasn't going to miss a moment of what was happening. At three o'clock, Grant's delegation rode toward the appointed spot. "Soon," Fred recalled, "a white flag appeared over the enemy's works, and a party of Confederates was seen approaching . . . and General Grant met his opponent."

Grant wrote of this meeting, "Pemberton and I had served in the same division during part of the Mexican War. I knew him well, therefore, and greeted him as an old acquaintance. He soon asked what terms I proposed to give his army if it surrendered. My answer was the same as proposed in my reply to his letter." Pemberton stiffened. He said that unconditional surrender was not acceptable and that he and his men would resume fighting. Grant wrote, "Pemberton then said, rather snappishly, 'The conference might as well end,' and turned abruptly as if to leave. I said, 'Very well.' "

But John Bowen, who was to die ten days later from his illness, stepped forward and convinced both parties to continue to talk. Though unstated, both sides knew that as long as Joe Johnston refused to fight, the North was assured of victory—yet a final battle would take many lives, both blue and gray. Some concessions by the North could end this now.

Pemberton and Grant talked informally while their respective staffs hammered out details of the surrender.

Grant agreed to let his staff and Pemberton's discuss terms of the surrender while he and Pemberton moved to the shade of a tree, where they exchanged small talk. When the officers signaled that they were finished, Grant told Pemberton as they parted that he would offer his final terms that evening.

Back in their own camps, both generals called together their most trusted advisers. At his father's side, Fred took in everything that was happening. He reported, "Father was immediately joined by the largest assemblage of generals and officers which I had ever seen—the heroes of the most brilliant campaign and siege recorded in the history of the world—deciding upon . . . the fate of their foes."

Just as Pemberton had suspected, having Vicksburg officially surrender on the Fourth of July pleased the Union officers. And they were sympathetic to Pemberton's request that the Confederate soldiers not be sent to prison. *Every* soldier dreaded the prisons, both North and South. Besides, transporting 30,000 men to prisons in the North would tie up trains, boats, and wagons needed elsewhere in the war effort.

Grant decided to offer Pemberton's men parole—which required them to sign an oath of allegiance to the United States government and state that they would not fight again. He knew the risk was that they would go join Joe Johnston, but he believed that most of these battle-weary men would just go home. Though he might draw criticism in the North for being this generous, he had respect for these defenders of Vicksburg. He didn't want to humiliate them. He also felt that they would be better citizens once the war was over if he treated them with some consideration now.

That evening, Grant sent Pemberton his final terms, which included the offer of parole. Then he waited for a reply. Fred was with his father. "I remained in the tent, sitting on my little cot, and feeling restless, but scarcely knowing why. Father sat at his writing table." Fred tried to be quiet as his father "began to write very hard, and with great interest in what he was writing." The minutes ticked by. When Fred thought he could stand it no longer, "at last there came an orderly with a dispatch."

Fred held his breath. He watched as his father "opened it, gave a sigh of relief, and said calmly, 'Vicksburg has surrendered.' I was thus the first to hear the news officially, announcing the fall of the Gibraltar of America, and, filled with enthusiasm, I ran out to spread the glad tidings. Officers rapidly assembled and there was a general rejoicing."

The forty-seven-day siege of Vicksburg was over.

✻ ✻ ✻

IN VICKSBURG ITSELF that evening of July 3, a Confederate officer stopped by the Lords' cave and told the family that General Bowen had gone to see Grant that day. Margaret Lord reported that everyone felt sick with anxiety and dread.

That same evening, Lucy, who knew nothing of what was happening, feared that the Yankees were preparing to storm the city. What else could the guns' silence mean? Mosquitoes whined in the hot, muggy darkness. Lucy wrote, "All was quiet. People could be seen walking around, concluding that the silence meant dreadful things on the morrow."

To her surprise, she saw her father, who had steadfastly refused to leave the family home, coming toward them. "We were all sitting outside the cave, twilight approaching, when Father came in sight," Lucy remembered. "Mother thought Father had decided to die with his family the next day, for everybody thought that General Grant would make the effort of his life to take the city on the 4th. Father came to mother, looking sad, with tears in his eyes, and said, 'You can all come home for a night's rest. General Pemberton has surrendered, and General Grant will enter the city in the morning.' "

And so, Lucy said, "We went home."

✻ ✻ ✻

DR. LORD WAS OUT AND ABOUT in the city the next morning when he learned the news. He returned quickly to his family's cave.

Mrs. Lord recalled that he was "pale as death and with such a look of agony on his face as I would wish never to see again." He told her, "Maggie, take the children home directly. The town is surrendered, and the Yankee army will enter at ten o'clock."

"I was speechless with grief," Mrs. Lord said. "No one spoke, even the poor children were silent, [and] all the weary way home I wept incessantly, meeting first one group of soldiers and then another, many of them with tears streaming down their faces."

The family had not left the area around their cave for weeks. As they walked home, they looked at the defeated town—at the craters in the streets, the torn-up sidewalks, flattened shrubbery and gardens, broken windows, and badly damaged or destroyed homes and businesses. Spent shells covered the ground. They were glad to see that the grand courthouse had suffered little damage, perhaps because captured Union officers had been held prisoner there, and when word of this had reached Admiral Porter, he made certain his cannon avoided it.

Finally the Lords made it to their home. Willie's mother never forgot it. "Such a scene of desolation you can hardly imagine . . . every room in the house injured and scarcely a window left whole."

More bad news awaited the family. They soon learned that everything they had stored at the Flowers plantation outside Vicksburg—furniture, other valuables, and Dr. Lord's vast collection of books—was lost. Willie reflected that had their possessions been stored in the church cellar, they probably would have been all right. Instead, one of Flowers' slaves later told the family how camp followers broke into the house and destroyed everything they couldn't carry with them. As for Dr. Lord's treasured books—Homer, Chaucer, Dante, Shakespeare, and more—a sad fate had befallen them.

"A huge plantation wagon was loaded with my father's invaluable library . . . and the contents were scattered upon the muddy road between the Flowers plantation and the Big Black River, so that for a mile and a half, as we were told, one might have walked on books."

✳ ✳ ✳

When Rebel soldiers surrendered their arms, Union soldiers watched respectfully.

AT TEN O'CLOCK on the morning of July 4, 1863, Confederate soldiers lined up, saluted the Confederate flag, and laid down their guns. Union soldiers, flush with victory, could have jeered. But none did. They stood by their trenches in silence, watching the thin, worn-out Rebels who had fought well and suffered gravely. Then one of the Northern boys started to clap. A few others joined in, and then more and more, until all up and down the line could be heard clapping, and then shouting, in recognition of a brave foe. At the tops of their voices, the boys in blue cheered themselves hoarse for the boys in gray. Breaking line, they came over to shake hands and to press food upon these defenders of Vicksburg who were enemies no more.

✳ ✳ ✳

IN TOWN, in front of their damaged home, Lucy and her brothers and parents watched the Confederate soldiers gathering for the formal surrender. Lucy wrote, "How sad was the spectacle that met our gaze; arms stacked in the center on the streets; men with tearful eyes and downcast faces walking here and there; men sitting in groups feeling that they would gladly have given their life-blood on the battlefield rather than hand over the guns and sabers so dear to them!"

Lucy watched as "the drummer-boy of a Tennessee regiment, rather than give up his drum, gave it to my brother, but it was very soon taken away from him . . . The instruments of the band of the Tennessee regiment were stacked in the middle of the street. Men looked so forlorn, some without any shoes, some with tattered garments, yet they would have fought on."

Like everyone in Vicksburg, she knew the town could not have held out much longer. Still, she reported, "men felt very bitterly toward General Pemberton because they were so determined that the place should not be taken on the Fourth and never dreamed that a surrender was ever thought of."

In 1865, when this photograph was taken, the Stars and Stripes had been flying over the Vicksburg courthouse for nearly two years, a painful sight for many in the city.

As townspeople watched, most from behind the curtains of their homes, they saw several units of Grant's army march into town accompanied by a band playing Northern patriotic songs. In her badly damaged house, Willie's mother reported, "You can imagine our feelings when the US Army entered, their banners flying and their hateful tunes sounding in our ears . . . You may be sure none of us raised our eyes to see the flag of the enemy in the place where our own had so proudly and defiantly waved so long."

The Union soldiers had waited for this moment when they would see their flag flying atop the grand courthouse. As they watched the Stars and Stripes replace the Confederate flag, they stood at attention and saluted with pride.

Then, just as the men who fought in the trenches had done, Union soldiers broke line and shared whatever they had with the Confederates. Grant arrived in the city a short time later and observed, "Our men had had full rations from the time the siege commenced, to the close. The enemy had been suffering, particularly towards the last. I myself saw our men taking bread from their haversacks, and giving it to the enemy they had so recently been engaged in starving out. It was accepted with . . . thanks."

Missouri was split in its support of the war and had troops fighting on both sides at Vicksburg. A Union captain from Hannibal, Missouri, recalled one particular incident that day in Vicksburg that he would never forget. One of his young soldiers had a brother in the Rebel army at Vicksburg. In town, the brothers spotted each other and fell out of ranks. Wrapping their arms around each other's waists, they walked together, one strong, in a fresh blue uniform, the other thin and weak, dressed in gray rags.

Union doctors set to work helping Confederate doctors with the sick and injured. Grant ordered that flour, coffee, sugar, tea, bacon, and other rations be distributed to townspeople, which drew them out of their homes and caves, in spite of their despair over what had happened. Then Grant went to the docks to personally greet Admiral Porter, who was bringing in all of his gunboats, rams, and transports to share the day's triumph. The two men grinned and firmly shook hands as they congratulated each other.

Over a year after Union officers first demanded the surrender of Vicksburg, the guns overlooking the Mississippi River were finally silent.

THE UNFINISHED WAR

July 1863 and Beyond

Newspapers in the North triumphantly reported the capture of Vicksburg, but the story was quickly overshadowed by the news out of Pennsylvania. The three-day battle of Gettysburg, which took over 50,000 lives, ended on July 3, 1863, the same day Pemberton and Grant negotiated the surrender of Vicksburg. Together the Confederacy's losses at Gettysburg and Vicksburg ensured that the North would win the war—though it would take another twenty-one months to stop the fighting.

✳ ✳ ✳

FOUR DAYS AFTER THE SURRENDER, Joe Johnston was on the run with Sherman's army in pursuit. Ultimately Sherman pulled back, for his troops were needed elsewhere. Some time later, because Johnston was his superior officer, Pemberton had to report to him. According to stories of that meeting, Johnston rose to greet him warmly as a friend, but Pemberton saluted stiffly, turned, and walked away. The two men would never meet again.

Some historians regard Grant's victory at Vicksburg at least in part as a result of Johnston's failure. Grant had his own view. He wrote, "Johnston evidently took in the situation and wisely, I think, abstained from making an assault on us because it would simply have inflicted loss on both sides without accomplishing any result."

✹ ✹ ✹

SHORTLY AFTER THE FALL OF VICKSBURG, Grant put Fred aboard a steamboat to St. Louis. He was worried about his son's health and wanted his wife to look after him. Though Fred's leg was at last healing and there was no longer a danger that it would have to be amputated, he was still sick with typhoid fever and dysentery—illnesses that had killed many soldiers. Julia Grant found expert medical care for him, and when Fred recovered, he accompanied his father to Washington, D.C. There he met Abraham Lincoln and saw his father receive a gold medal from Congress for his conquest of Vicksburg. Fred glowed with pride as people clamored to meet the famous general, cheering him wherever he went, but he saw how uncomfortable this attention made his father. The modest Grant told his wife, "Really, it was very embarrassing. I heartily wished myself back in camp."

Grant returned to Vicksburg to oversee the occupation of the city and the orderly processing of the surrendered Confederates. Julia, Fred, and the three other children joined him, and they lived for a while in an elegant mansion high in the Vicksburg hills that had sustained little damage during the siege. Other Union generals also selected private homes for

Union general James McPherson (seated second from right) is shown with his staff outside the Balfour home where he headquartered during the occupation.

their personal use, sometimes ejecting the owners. Emma Balfour and her family had to share their home with General James Birdseye McPherson and his family. To regain the citizenship they lost when the South seceded from the United States, men in the community were required to sign a loyalty oath to the United States government. (Women were exempted from this since they did not have the right to vote.) Dr. Balfour refused to sign the hated oath, and as a result he was under constant surveillance and subjected to military harassment. More than once he was ordered to give money to Union sympathizers.

About 700 of Pemberton's men also refused to take the oath, a requirement for parole, so they went to prison. A nineteen-year-old Confederate soldier who was leaving for a prison camp in the North wrote: "I stopped and looked back at the crestfallen city of Vicksburg . . . and thought of how many months we had nobly held the place against all the efforts of the Yankee nation, and bore privations and hardships of all kinds. Tears rose to my eyes and my very heart swelled with emotion. Being a prisoner did not in the least affect me, but the loss of the place, which was such a great downfall to the Confederacy . . . caused me much pain."

Mary Loughborough's husband also chose prison, and Mary moved to St. Louis to be closer to him. Boarding a steamboat with her small daughter, she knew she would miss the city she was leaving behind. "Vicksburg, with her terraced hills, with her pleasant homes and sad memories, passed from my view in the gathering twilight," she wrote, "passed, but the river flowed on the same."

✳ ✳ ✳

GRANT WANTED TO RESTORE ORDER to the community as quickly as possible. He imposed martial law and a strict curfew. Freedom of speech was curtailed, and people were readily arrested and jailed for minor offenses. Only citizens who signed the loyalty oath could hold jobs and operate businesses. Those who refused to sign had to obtain a pass to go anywhere outside town. They could even be banished from the city for a year if they made threats against the United States government or insulted Federal officers. In one incident, five women were banished after walking out of a church service rather than participate in a prayer for President Lincoln.

The Union occupation army of 7,500 soldiers was kept busy. According to Willie Lord, Grant was "a popular conquering general. He suppressed with an iron hand looting, violence and vandalism." Townspeople appreciated that, but some were concerned about black soldiers helping to patrol the city. They worried that these former slaves might retaliate against whites for the injustices of slavery. They soon realized, however, that white soldiers caused as many problems as blacks. Willie's mother, for one, had no use for any Yankee. She had a run-in one day with several Union soldiers who, for sport, had turned over her filled laundry basket when she was hanging clothes on the line. She confronted them angrily: "I should think soldiers would have too much feeling in this hour of our distress to intrude even to the privacy of a lady's home."

They pointed to the badly damaged church rectory and sneered, "Do you call this a lady's home? You ought to keep it in better order." Margaret

When Vicksburg surrendered, the Union put confiscated cannon and artillery into service against the South.

Lord was livid. "It is all you have left to us for a home," she declared, "and I will tell you now that I have lived for months in the midst of thirty-thousand Confederate soldiers and this is the first insult I have ever received."

After years of war, few Southerners had enough money to pay wages to their former slaves in exchange for their help, so, like Margaret Lord, they now did their own work. Some plantation and farm wives, whose husbands had not yet returned from the war or were dead, had to learn how to grow crops. Many mothers and their children were plunged into poverty, and women did whatever they could to earn money, from taking in sewing to teaching school or selling eggs. Some of them turned their homes into boardinghouses. Others competed with former slaves for any menial tasks that would pay a little something. Vicksburg overflowed with homeless people. The Union army had so wasted the countryside that after the siege, hunger forced an estimated 25,000 people, including freed slaves and camp followers, into the city so they could receive Union army rations. Housing was almost nonexistent, so people set up makeshift camps. In the unrelenting summer heat, the air so thick with humidity that it was hard to breathe, disease was rampant and many died.

Officially only a dozen civilians had been killed and about fifty injured in the siege, but in the next few years many more died, some of them from lung problems related to the dampness in the caves, or exposure to the caustic powder in the shells that had exploded around them for forty-seven days. When Mark Twain interviewed survivors a few years later, one of them said about his friends, "Hunger and misery and sickness and fright and sorrow, and I don't know what all, got so loaded into them that none of them were ever rightly their old selves after the siege. They all died but three of us within a couple of years."

In the weeks and months following the siege, Vicksburg trudged a slow road to recovery. Townspeople cleaned up the debris and filled in the caves or boarded them up. They repaired their homes and businesses. After the war, faced with high property taxes, many lost their homes when they could not pay them. Some homes were eventually torn down because of neglect, and the city never recovered its pre-war glory.

✳ ✳ ✳

FRED GRANT ATTENDED a private school in New Jersey the year following the siege. During one of his breaks he went to visit his father, then stationed in Virginia, where the war was still being fought. Dressed in his gray and black school uniform, he was duck hunting in a small boat on the James River when he passed a Union gunboat. It fired on him and ordered him to surrender. He was brought aboard, and, according to his mother, "had some trouble in convincing his captors that he was not an enemy though he wore the gray, but the son of their General Grant."

Lucy McRae also returned to school, but in Vicksburg at the all-girls academy she had previously attended. Vicksburg became a busy Union port and Yankee soldiers were everywhere, including Sky Parlor Hill, where off-duty soldiers liked to watch the barges, steamboats, and ironclads coming and going on the river.

Lucy watched, too, but from the safety of the upper porch of her home. Her brother John had survived the siege of Vicksburg. It was not until many months later, when he finally returned to them, that she and her family knew that her oldest brother, Allen, was also safe. He had been stationed a thousand miles away, assigned to help protect Jefferson Davis. Lucy wrote that Allen "was the last man who stood guard at President Davis' tent, and when discharged by him, was given a letter, a horse and a $20 gold piece. My brother rode from Virginia on that horse, carrying the gold piece in the bottom of his boot."

Shortly after the siege ended, the Lords decided to leave Vicksburg. They could have gone to St. Louis to stay with Dr. Lord's brother, a prominent judge. Indeed, General Grant, who knew the judge, offered Dr. Lord written permission to cross through Federal lines. But the Reverend was still committed to the Southern cause. He asked instead for passage by riverboat deeper into the South so he could continue his work as a Confederate army chaplain. Willie reported that General Grant agreed, for he "admired courageous persistence in the fulfillment of duty."

The Lords dug up the family silver they had buried in the churchyard before the start of the siege and converted the rest of their belongings into Confederate money (which soon became worthless). Willie wrote of their emotional departure from Vicksburg, "As we stepped aboard the boat which was to bear us on toward the unknown experiences that awaited us during the death struggles of the Confederacy, a group of our loving friends and my father's devoted parishioners waved us a sad farewell . . . and we became . . . refugees adrift upon the hopeless current of a losing Cause."

✸ ✸ ✸

WHEN THE CIVIL WAR officially ended in April 1865, much of the South lay in ruins. In describing the desolation of towns burned and

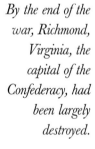

By the end of the war, Richmond, Virginia, the capital of the Confederacy, had been largely destroyed.

plantations deserted, a woman spoke of having no future and no hope. Southerners, she said, were exiles in their own land. Returning soldiers found their homes destroyed and their families displaced. Some soldiers were emotionally traumatized by the horrors they'd witnessed and would never be the same. Many more were suffering from disease or injuries—in Mississippi alone in the year following the war, twenty percent of the state budget went to the purchase of artificial arms and legs for veterans.

Most Southern boys and men who had signed up to fight weren't trying to defend slavery. They'd grown up in a culture that believed blacks to be inferior, but only ten percent of them came from slave-owning families. Instead, they marched off to war because they supported states' rights, or because they were determined to defend their homeland. Some went because they were loyal to the South, others because they would be accused of being cowardly if they didn't. They became soldiers because they were drafted or needed a steady paycheck or wanted the adventure.

None of them could have known what they were getting into. When it was over, almost all would have agreed with the Vicksburg resident who declared, "I never want to live through another war, never, never."

Left: Young Southern recruits in Virginia, before the war started.

Right: Seasoned Union soldiers at the Battle of Chancellorsville in 1863.

AFTERWORD

Postscripts

The Lord family left Vicksburg for Mobile, Alabama, and then moved to Charleston, South Carolina. They fled Charleston when General Sherman and his army arrived. After the war they returned to Vicksburg and lived there a number of years before moving to New York, where they were originally from. Dr. Lord led a congregation in Cooperstown. Willie is buried in a local cemetery near his parents. Unfortunately, while one photo of Dr. Lord exists and is in this book, there are no known photos of Willie and the entire Lord family.

Lucy McRae continued to live in Vicksburg. When she married, she moved to Lewisburg, West Virginia, and mothered one daughter, also named Lucy. She died in 1930 and is buried in Lewisburg.

The McRaes' country home at Bolton's Depot, where Lucy and her family stayed before the siege started, was in the direct path of Union troops and was destroyed by them. But Lucy's wartime home still stands in Vicksburg today, and one can imagine her as a child on the upper porch, looking out at the river.

Rice and Mary Ann, the McRaes' two house slaves, gained their freedom. There are no records of what became of either of them after they left the McRae family. Some freed slaves moved to the North to look for work. Others went west to become homesteaders or even moved to other countries. Some blacks joined the military and served out West in the campaigns against Native Americans. But like whites, most blacks stayed and tried to rebuild their lives. Some continued to work for the families they had served—but for pay.

Frederick Grant attended West Point and spent much of his career in the military, where he rose to the rank of general. He served as his father's secretary while Grant was president, was later the ambassador to Austria-Hungary, and for two years was police commissioner of New York City. In his memoirs, Grant wrote of Fred at Vicksburg, "My son accompanied me throughout the campaign and siege, and caused no anxiety either to me or to his mother, who was at home. He looked out for himself and was in every battle of the campaign. His age . . . enabled him to take in all he saw, and to retain a recollection of it that would not be possible in more mature years."

Ulysses S. Grant became a national hero when Vicksburg fell. He assumed command of all Union forces, and it was he who accepted Robert E. Lee's surrender at Appomattox on April 9, 1865, ending the war. He was president of the United States from 1868 to 1876.

William Tecumseh Sherman's wife, two daughters, and two sons joined him in Vicksburg during the first months of the occupation. His older son, Willy, was eleven. Like Fred Grant, he had his own Federal uniform and wanted to be a soldier. Months later the boy was dead from yellow fever. A grieving Sherman would write of this loss, "I could not leave my post, and sent for the family to come to me in that fatal climate and in that sickly period of the year, and behold the result!"

Sherman is most often remembered for his brutal march through the South and the capture of Atlanta, events that laid waste to the South and helped end the war. He succeeded Grant as commander of the army.

John Pemberton, as he himself predicted, was blamed by many for the loss of Vicksburg. Once he surrendered the city, he accepted a reduction in rank and continued to serve in the war as a colonel. For a while he was on Robert E. Lee's staff. Lee always addressed him as "General" and sought his opinion on important matters. When the war was over, Pemberton wanted a court of inquiry into his role at Vicksburg but was never given one. He and Johnston continued pointing fingers of blame at each other for decades.

Joe Johnston retained his command in the Confederacy, in spite of his refusal to come to Vicksburg's aid. He was often reviled for his recurring pattern of refusing to fight. He and Sherman became friends after the war, and Johnston served as an honorary pallbearer at Sherman's funeral.

Jefferson Davis, president of the Confederate States, was held responsible for the war and imprisoned in solitary confinement for two and a half years. He lived to be eighty and published a two-volume history of the Civil War written from a Southern perspective. It became a bestseller in the South. After his death, his wife lived in New York City and became friends with another widow, Julia Grant. When Mrs. Davis died, Fred Grant arranged for a United States Army band to play Southern songs and accompany her casket to the train station. She was taken to Richmond, Virginia, and buried next to her husband.

Old Abe, the American bald eagle who was the mascot for the 8th Wisconsin Infantry, was at Vicksburg during the entire campaign. After the war he was named an honorary citizen of Wisconsin and gave his name to the 101st Airborne Division, United States Army, known as the Screaming Eagles. He lived out his life in a special room in the Wisconsin state capitol. The top of the Wisconsin monument at the Vicksburg National Military Park features a six-foot statute of Old Abe.

Orion Howe, the fourteen-year-old Union drummer boy from Illinois who bravely ran through deadly fire to get more ammunition for his regiment, recovered from his serious wound. He was later awarded the Medal of Honor for his service at Vicksburg—one of the youngest soldiers ever to receive it.

Mary Loughborough's husband survived prison, and the family settled in Little Rock, Arkansas. After the war, Mary published her journal, titling it *My Cave Life in Vicksburg*. It was popular with Northern readers. She later founded a women's magazine called *Southern Ladies' Journal*. Her husband died shortly after their fourth child was born. Mary's health was adversely affected by her time living in a cave during the siege, and she died in 1887 at age fifty.

Emma Balfour also died in 1887. She had already outlived her husband by a decade. She never left Vicksburg. In her will she remembered her favorite house slave, Margaret Ann, whose wedding she had hosted in her home.

Vicksburg is now a city of 26,000 residents, both black and white. Several elegant homes that survived the siege are either bed and breakfast inns or are open for tours. In addition to Lucy's home, visitors can see Christ Episcopal Church, where Dr. Lord preached daily during the siege. But the rectory next to the church, where the Lord family lived, was torn down because of extensive damage. The courthouse is now the Old Courthouse Museum and is considered one of the best Confederate museums in the South. It has many exhibits on the siege, and hanging in a place of honor is an oil painting of General Pemberton.

Congress kept the South under military rule for more than a decade following the war. Federal troops were present in Vicksburg a full thirteen years—longer than the United States occupation of Germany after World War II.

For eighty-four years following Vicksburg's surrender, proud citizens resisted any organized celebration of the Fourth of July. Only in 1947, when General Dwight D. Eisenhower of World War II fame came to visit, did the city put on a celebration worthy of the great American war hero. Since then, while they have not forgotten their history and readily share it with visitors, Vicksburg residents have celebrated Independence Day with the rest of the country.

Sky Parlor Hill ceased to exist in the years following the war when it was graded down to make way for new construction.

Vicksburg National Military Park was created by an act of Congress in 1899. It is the final resting place for 17,000 Union soldiers. Of that number, 13,000 are in unmarked graves since Civil War soldiers did not carry identifying information like the dog tags that today's soldiers wear. There are no Confederate graves in the park; since the Rebels were not considered United States citizens when they died, by law they could not be buried on federal property. Even without them, the park is one of the largest Civil War cemeteries in the country.

Visitors to the park can see miles of reconstructed trenches, a Union tunnel, and a collection of cannon and other weapons. When Civil War reenactors are present, they help visitors imagine what the siege was like.

On display is the Union ironclad gunboat *Cairo*, which was sunk by the Confederates in December 1862 and later salvaged. Also of interest are the 1,248 monuments erected by both Union and Confederate troops who served at Vicksburg. These monuments honor soldiers from twenty-eight states who sent troops to fight at Vicksburg (there were thirty-four states at the time). Each is unique and each is made of the state's native stone.

Illinois had the most soldiers at Vicksburg—over 36,000—and has the largest monument. It has forty-seven steps, one for each day of the siege. Missouri has the only monument dedicated to soldiers on both sides, commemorating its native sons who fought against each other at Vicksburg.

Facts About the War

✳ Forty thousand Confederate and Union soldiers are estimated to have perished from wounds or illness during the entire Vicksburg campaign. The siege itself claimed almost 3,000 Confederate soldiers and 4,900 Federal soldiers.

✳ The American population at the time of the war was 30 million. The Union army had between 2.5 and 2.75 million men in uniform, while the less populated South had 750,000 to 1.23 million. The figure usually given for the number of soldiers who died in the Civil War is 620,000 (more than the combined deaths of all other American wars). But if you count the number of men who subsequently died of injuries or illness inflicted during the Civil War, the figure might be as high as 1.5 million. Because regiments were made up of soldiers from the same area, in one battle some small towns lost most or even all of their men and boys between the ages of fifteen and fifty. Many of these solders were buried in unmarked graves, far from home and lost to their families forever.

✳ The Union awarded 128 Medals of Honor to Union soldiers who fought at Vicksburg.

✳ Vicksburg had the most elaborate trench system ever devised prior to World War I.

✷ The typical Civil War soldier was twenty-six years old; stood five feet, eight inches tall; and weighed 135 pounds.

✷ Few regular soldiers in either the North or the South had military experience prior to the war, and they received little more than basic training before seeing actual combat. Most volunteer soldiers were farmers and small business owners, and it's possible that as many as 400,000 were boys under the age of eighteen. Though post-traumatic stress disorder was not a known diagnosis at the time, many soldiers who returned home from the war suffered from depression and nightmares and could not resume normal lives.

✷ During the war, it was not unusual for officers to bring their wives and children with them or at least to have visits from them. Some soldiers also had their families with them, living alongside the army wherever it went.

✷ The Union armies were named for rivers, and the Rebel armies for states. Thus, Grant's Army of the Tennessee was so named because the men were on the Tennessee River when it was organized, while one of the Southern armies was the Army of Northern Virginia because that's where it was organized.

In spite of primitive living conditions, families sometimes accompanied soldiers to war.

Children Orphaned by the War

Tens of thousands of children lost their fathers in the Civil War. If they subsequently lost their mothers and did not have relatives to take over, they faced great difficulty. Responses to this problem varied from place to place. The state of Pennsylvania lost 50,000 soldiers in the war and established orphanages and schools for its fatherless children. The Cleveland Jewish Orphan Asylum opened in 1868 for Jewish children who were orphaned by the war. The Kentucky Female Orphan School in Midway cared for forty-six girls in 1858. By 1871, that number had doubled because of war orphans. Churches and other religious groups set up homes and orphanages across the country in the post-war years, and some orphaned or half-orphaned children—many of whom lost their fathers in the Civil War—rode orphan trains from one place to another in search of new families.

Women and the War

When men went off to war, many women had to take over their roles at home. To help with the war effort, women all over the country pitched in to do what they could. They knitted socks, made clothing and quilts, and gathered and shipped supplies like blankets and towels, soap, rifle cartridges, writing paper, Bibles, and food. They held fund-raisers and often donated personal possessions, or sold them and donated the money. They visited army camps and prisons. They wrote letters to lonely soldiers or helped wounded soldiers write to loved ones.

Religious Sisters left their convents to help nurse the ill and wounded, often traveling long distances. Some died on battlefields. Many were overworked and hungry. In Vicksburg, the Sisters of Mercy moved about the city even though they were in direct danger from the shelling. Because of this, their bishop asked that they travel separately, concerned that they could all be killed in a single explosion.

While 2,000 women are thought to have been nurses in both the North and South during the war, countless others volunteered in hospitals

Jennie Hodgers (right) disguised herself as a man and fought at Vicksburg.

and military camps and took the sick and injured into their own homes. Both Dorothea Dix and Clara Barton, who helped nurse wounded soldiers, led efforts to organize their care.

An estimated 600 women dressed in uniform and passed as men to fight alongside their male comrades. A woman named Jennie Irene Hodgers gave herself the name of Albert Cashier and fought with the Union army at Vicksburg. Disguised as a man, she was considered a brave and dependable soldier. When her identity as a woman was discovered many years after the war ended, her fellow soldiers convinced the United States Pension Bureau to drop charges that she had defrauded the government—an action that allowed her to continue receiving a military pension.

Reconstruction

Both before and after the war, the South's economy was based on agriculture. After the war ended, large landowners could not afford to hire all the workers they needed to replace their former slaves, and those former slaves and returning small farmers could not afford to buy land. This led to the system known as sharecropping, where poor farmers "leased" land from plantation owners in return for a share of their crops. This worked well for landowners, but because of unfair business practices, many sharecroppers became the poorest of the poor. Freed blacks likened sharecropping to slavery, for even though they could not be whipped or sold, they were enslaved by debt. Many sharecroppers, both black and white, lived on their "leased" land for generations, remaining poor and uneducated.

    The Thirteenth Amendment to the Constitution outlawed slavery in 1865. This and other new laws were meant to ensure that blacks became full citizens. They could now go to school, and black males could vote. Some whites blamed blacks for the poverty and violence that plagued Southern society. Whites who supported black advancement found themselves in conflict with whites who refused to accept blacks as equals.

Some Southern states passed what became known as the Black Laws in the early years after the war, followed two decades later by the Jim Crow Laws, all of which were meant to make blacks second-class citizens without the right to vote. A policy of "separate but equal" was used to institute widespread segregation in education and in society. Segregation did indeed separate the races, but it did not make things equal. Blacks had to use their own drinking fountains, rest rooms, and swimming pools. They were told to sit at the back of public buses and in special cars on trains, and they were denied service in many restaurants and hotels. Segregation was also widespread in some Northern states.

Terror groups like the Ku Klux Klan sprang up to keep both blacks and whites too frightened to challenge segregation laws and racial codes. Blacks who asserted their rights risked being the targets of violence. While there were pockets of progress—Vicksburg briefly had a black mayor and a black sheriff, and the state of Mississippi sent the first black senator to the United States Senate—these advancements did not last.

Not until the civil rights movement of the 1960s did the nation finally begin to successfully reverse racism. Today, full racial justice is still not a reality in America.

FOR MORE ABOUT THE CIVIL WAR

Books

The Boys' War by Jim Murphy (New York: Clarion Books, 1990) gives voice to the experiences of the as many as 400,000 youths sixteen and younger who may have served in the Civil War. *Civil War A–Z* by Norman Bolotin (New York: Dutton Children's Books, 2002) presents an overview of the war and its most important places, events, and people. *Fields of Fury: The American Civil War* by James M. McPherson (New York: Atheneum Books for Young Readers, 2002) is a well-written history of the war, rich with illustration.  *Life Goes On: The Civil War at Home 1861–1865* by James R. Arnold and Roberta Wiener (Minneapolis: Lerner Publications, 2002) considers how the war affected everyone, with emphasis on the burden placed on women. In *Life in the South During the Civil War* (San Diego, California: Lucent Books, 1997), James P. Reger considers the day-to-day lives of everyone from slaves to middle-class farmers to wealthy planters.

Slavery and the Coming of the Civil War: 1831–1861 by Christopher Collier and James Lincoln Collier (New York: Benchmark Books, 2000) offers a look inside the institution of slavery and what it was like for the people who lived it.

Documentary Film

The Civil War, from Ken Burns, is an ambitious eleven-hour undertaking, rich with the voices of those who were there, illustrated with black-and-white photographs, and accompanied by period music.

Websites

www.nps.gov/vick is part of the website for the National Parks Service and offers information about the Vicksburg Military Park and the history of the siege.

www.vicksburgcvb.org shows glimpses of the city and some of its historic buildings.

www.oldcourthouse.org features Civil War–era photographs of Vicksburg.

www.AmericanCivilWar.com is a useful website offering extensive information about the history of the Civil War, including maps and photographs.

www.historyplace.com offers an overview of the war and information about specific battles.

SELECTED BIBLIOGRAPHY

Both Willie Lord and Lucy McRae wrote of their childhood experiences for *Harper's Magazine*, Willie in December 1908 and Lucy in June 1912. Their articles were reprinted in *Yankee Bullets, Rebel Rations* by Gordon A. Cotton (Vicksburg, Mississippi: The Print Shop, 2003). Frederick Grant was interviewed by or wrote several times for publications about his experiences at Vicksburg. This material is part of the archives of the Ulysses S. Grant Association, Southern Illinois University, Carbondale, Illinois.

Arnold, James R. *Grant Wins the War: Decision at Vicksburg.* New York: John Wiley & Sons, 1997.

Balfour, Emma. *Vicksburg: A City Under Siege; The Diary of Emma Balfour.* Compiled by Phillip C. Weinberger, 1983 (no additional publication information).

Confederate Women. Edited by Mauriel Phillips Joslyn. Gretna, Louisiana: Pelican Publishing Company, Inc., 1996.

Cotton, Gordon A. *Vicksburg: Southern Stories of the Siege.* Vicksburg, Mississippi: The Print Shop, 1988.

———. *Yankee Bullets, Rebel Rations.* Vicksburg, Mississippi: The Print Shop, 2003.

———, and Ralph C. Mason. *With Malice Toward Some: The Military Occupation of Vicksburg, 1864–1895.* Vicksburg, Mississippi: Vicksburg and Warren County Historical Society, 1991.

Flood, Charles Bracelen. *Grant and Sherman: The Friendship That Won the Civil War.* New York: Farrar, Straus and Giroux, 2005.

Foote, Shelby. *The Beleaguered City: The Vicksburg Campaign.* New York: The Modern Library, 1995.

Graham, Martin F., Richard A. Saurs, and George Skoch. *The Blue and the Gray: The Conflict Between North and South.* Lincolnwood, Illinois: Publications International Ltd., 1997.

Grant, Frederick Dent. "General Frederick Dent Grant: Recollections of His Famous Father." 1908 interview by James B. Morrow. Reprinted in the *Ulysses S. Grant Association Newsletter* (Southern Illinois University, Carbondale) 9, no. 2 (January 1972).

———. "An Interview With Colonel Frederick D. Grant About His Father." Interview by A. E. Watrous. Originally printed in *McClure's Magazine,* May 1984. Reprinted in the *Ulysses S. Grant Association Newsletter* (Southern Illinois University, Carbondale) 7, no. 4 (July 1970).

———. "Reminiscences of General Frederick Dent Grant." Compiled and printed in the *Ulysses S. Grant Association Newsletter* (Southern Illinois University, Carbondale) 6, no. 3 (April 1969).

———. "With Grant at Vicksburg." Originally printed in *The Outlook,* July 2, 1898, and reprinted in the *Ulysses S. Grant Association Newsletter* (Southern Illinois University, Carbondale) 7, no. 1 (October 1969).

Grant, Julia. *The Personal Memoirs of Julia Dent Grant.* Edited by John Y. Simon. New York: G. P. Putnam's Sons, 1975.

Grant, U. S. *Personal Memoirs of U. S. Grant.* New York: Da Capo Press, 1982.

Hankinson, Alan. *Vicksburg 1863: Grant Clears the Mississippi.* Oxford, England: Osprey Publishing, 2002.

Hoehling, A. A. *Vicksburg: 47 Days of Siege.* Mechanicsburg, Pennsylvania: Stackpole Books, 1969.

Kennett, Lee. *Sherman: A Soldier's Life.* New York: HarperCollins Publishers, 2001.

Korn, Jerry. *War on the Mississippi: Grant's Vicksburg Campaign.* Chicago: Time-Life Books, 1985.

Lord, Mrs. W. W. *Journal Kept by Mrs. W. W. Lord During the Siege of Vicksburg by the Forces of General U. S. Grant, May and July, 1863.* Springfield, Massachusetts: Connecticut Valley Historical Society, no date. Manuscript Division, Library of Congress.

Loughborough, Mary. *My Cave Life in Vicksburg.* New York: D. Appleton and Company, 1864.

Marten, James. *The Children's Civil War.* Chapel Hill: The University of North Carolina Press, 1998.

Schultz, Duane. *The Most Glorious Fourth: Vicksburg and Gettysburg, July 4, 1863.* New York: W. W. Norton & Company, 2002.

Sherman, W. T. *Sherman: Memoirs of General W. T. Sherman.* Bloomington: Indiana University Press, 1957.

Twain, Mark. *Cave Life During the Siege of Vicksburg.* Pamphlet, Vicksburg Military Park.

Waldrep, Christopher. *Vicksburg's Long Shadow: The Civil War Legacy of Race and Remembrance.* Lanham, Maryland: Littlefield Publishers, 2005.

Werner, Emmy E. *Reluctant Witnesses: Children's Voices from the Civil War.* Boulder, Colorado: Westview Press, 1998.

Wheeler, Richard. *The Siege of Vicksburg.* New York: HarperCollins Publishers, 1991.

Winschel, Terrence J. *Vicksburg: Fall of the Confederate Gibraltar.* Abilene, Texas: McWhiney Foundation Press, 1999.

ENDNOTES

Introduction
4 "Although I was only": Cotton, *Yankee Bullets*, p. 65.

Chapter 1: War Comes to Vicksburg
11 "a place of education": Cotton, *Yankee Bullets*, p. 65.
14 "Vicksburg is the key": Winschel, *Vicksburg: Fall*, p. 14.
14–15 "Mississippians don't know": Korn, *War on the Mississippi*, p. 19.
17 "One bright afternoon": Cotton, *Yankee Bullets*, p. 65.

Chapter 2: The Christmas Eve Ball
23 "Great God, Phil": Korn, *War on the Mississippi*, p. 63.
24 "The party is at an end": Korn, *War on the Mississippi*, p. 63.
25 "He mounts a breastwork": Wheeler, *The Siege of Vicksburg*, p. 91.
26 "I reached Vicksburg at the time": Hoehling, *Vicksburg: 47 Days*, p. 4.

Chapter 3: The General's Boy Goes to War
27 "Whenever she could": Frederick Grant, "Recollections," p. 4.
27 "I, being the eldest": Frederick Grant, "Reminiscences," p. 4.

27 "I considered it": Julia Grant, *The Personal Memoirs*, p. 92.

28 "We may have some fighting": Julia Grant, *The Personal Memoirs*, p. 92.

32 "I cannot spare this man": Schultz, *The Most Glorious Fourth*, p. 31.

32 "Somehow he was more partner": Schultz, *The Most Glorious Fourth*, p. 134.

34–35 "the General was greatly amused": Julia Grant, *The Personal Memoirs*, p. 111.

37 "the river was lighted up": Frederick Grant, "With Grant at Vicksburg," p. 2.

37 "Indeed, it was a grand sight": Julia Grant, *The Personal Memoirs*, p. 112.

37 "was quietly smoking": Frederick Grant, "With Grant at Vicksburg," p. 2.

37 "magnificent, but terrible": U. S. Grant, *Personal Memoirs of U. S. Grant*, p. 241.

37 "It was as if hell": Korn, *War on the Mississippi*, p. 85.

37–38 "The batteries were passed": Julia Grant, *The Personal Memoirs*, p. 112.

Chapter 4: Burying the Family Silver

40 "With the deep but muffled boom": Cotton, *Yankee Bullets*, p. 21.

41 "How is it possible you live here?": Loughborough, *My Cave Life*, p. 12.

42 "I looked over this beautiful landscape": Loughborough, *My Cave Life*, p. 12.

42 "Resting in Vicksburg": Loughborough, *My Cave Life*, p. 12.

42 "I sprang from my bed": Loughborough, *My Cave Life*, p. 15.

42–43 "While I hesitated": Loughborough, *My Cave Life*, p. 16.

43 "We remained on the veranda": Loughborough, *My Cave Life*, p. 18.

43 "the glad sound of the whistle": Loughborough, *My Cave Life*, p. 23.

44 "our entire household": Cotton, *Yankee Bullets*, p. 21.

44 "a planter's cordial welcome": Cotton, *Yankee Bullets*, p. 22.

Chapter 5: At the Battle Front

45 "I was to remain": Frederick Grant, "Recollections," p. 4.

46 "I asked General Thomas to let me": Frederick Grant, "Recollections," p. 4.

46 "my guilty conscience": Frederick Grant, "With Grant at Vicksburg," p. 3.

47 "the horrors of a battlefield": Frederick Grant, "Recollections," p. 3.

47 "Night came on and": Frederick Grant, "Recollections," p. 5.

47 "I followed four soldiers": Frederick Grant, "Recollections," p. 5.

47 "Surgeons were tossing": Frederick Grant, "Recollections," p. 5.

47–48 "I picked my way among": Frederick Grant, "Recollections," p. 5.

48 "Why, hello, is that": Frederick Grant, "With Grant at Vicksburg," p. 3.

48 "About fifty yards off": Frederick Grant, "With Grant at Vicksburg," p. 3.

49 "where some officers were": Frederick Grant, "With Grant at Vicksburg," p. 3.

49 "Father, who was ever kind": Frederick Grant, "With Grant at Vicksburg," p. 3.

49 "we conceived the idea": Frederick Grant, "With Grant at Vicksburg," p. 4.

50 "I, for one, did not propose": Frederick Grant, "With Grant at Vicksburg," p. 4.

50 "without a tent, in the midst": Korn, *War on the Mississippi*, p. 109.

51 "and here again I saw": Frederick Grant, "With Grant at Vicksburg," p. 4.

51–52 "the enemy's sharpshooters": Frederick Grant, "With Grant at Vicksburg," p. 4.

52 "Confederate troops passed": Frederick Grant, "With Grant at Vicksburg," p. 4.

52 "a mounted officer with": Frederick Grant, "With Grant at Vicksburg," p. 4.

53 "I saw the match put": Frederick Grant, "Recollections," p. 6.

Chapter 6: The Yankees Are Coming!

54 "We were in far more danger": Loughborough, *My Cave Life*, p. 27.

54 "May I not be in danger": Loughborough, *My Cave Life*, p. 27.

55 "Very hurriedly we made our": Loughborough, *My Cave Life*, p. 27.

55 "was crowded with crushing": Loughborough, *My Cave Life*, p. 28.

55 "With our sewing": Loughborough, *My Cave Life*, p. 35.

56 "their arms were filled": Cotton, *Yankee Bullets*, p. 39.

58 "My mother was so constituted": Cotton, *Yankee Bullets*, p. 22.

58 "reluctantly gave his consent": Cotton, *Yankee Bullets*, p. 22.

58 "On our return journey": Cotton, *Yankee Bullets*, p. 22.

59 "My mother, so comfortably": Cotton, *Yankee Bullets*, p. 66.

59 "I remember so well how": Cotton, *Yankee Bullets*, p. 66.

60 "When we drove into": Cotton, *Yankee Bullets*, p. 66.

60 "there were no pickets": Cotton, *Yankee Bullets*, p. 67.

Chapter 7: The Road to Vicksburg

61 "This I thought of all": Wheeler, *The Siege of Vicksburg*, p. 27.

63–64 "Our line broke": Frederick Grant, "With Grant at Vicksburg," p. 5.

65 "While a battle is raging": U. S. Grant, *Personal Memoirs of U. S. Grant*, p. 272.

65 "We killed each other": Korn, *War on the Mississippi*, p. 119.

65–66 "I became enthused": Frederick Grant, "With Grant at Vicksburg," p. 5.

66 "Following the retreating": Frederick Grant, "With Grant at Vicksburg," p. 5.

66 "came dashing up": Frederick Grant, "With Grant at Vicksburg," p. 5.

67 "After dark, the whole scene": Schultz, *The Most Glorious Fourth*, p. 101.

68 "Until this moment I never": Hoehling, *Vicksburg: 47 Days*, p. 8.

Chapter 8: Enemy at the Gates

69 "passed groups of anxious": Loughborough, *My Cave Life*, p. 41.

70 "Where on earth": Loughborough, *My Cave Life*, p. 43.

70 "Afterward we were told": Loughborough, *My Cave Life*, p. 45.

71 "From twelve o'clock": Balfour, *Vicksburg: A City*, p. 3.

71–72 "I had everything that": Balfour, *Vicksburg: A City*, p. 3.

72 "the ladies waved": Loughborough, *My Cave Life*, p. 47.

72 "What a sad evening": Loughborough, *My Cave Life*, p. 47.

73 "I still conceive [Vicksburg] to be": Schultz, *The Most Glorious Fourth*, p. 103.

73 "I have decided to hold": Schultz, *The Most Glorious Fourth*, p. 103.

74 "A long line of high": Schultz, *The Most Glorious Fourth*, p. 105.

75 "At every point": Sherman, *Memoirs of General W. T. Sherman*, p. 326.

75 "This is a death struggle": Korn, *War on the Mississippi*, p. 127.

75 "The excitement was intense": Loughborough, *My Cave Life*, p. 50.

76–77 "We ran to the small cave": Loughborough, *My Cave Life*, p. 56.

77 "The boys were": Hoehling, *Vicksburg: 47 Days*, p. 36.

77–78 "We fixed bayonets": Hoehling, *Vicksburg: 47 Days*, p. 38.

78 "had a narrow escape": Frederick Grant, "With Grant at Vicksburg," p. 6.

78 "with blood streaming": Frederick Grant, "With Grant at Vicksburg," p. 6.

79–80 "All the soldiers came out": Wheeler, *The Siege of Vicksburg*, p. 176.

Chapter 9: Into the Caves

82 "a bombshell burst into": Schultz, *The Most Glorious Fourth*, p. 126.

83 "any one of them should collapse": Cotton, *Yankee Bullets*, p. 22.

83 "children played while": Cotton, *Yankee Bullets*, p. 23.

84 "It was living like plant roots": Hankinson, *Vicksburg 1863*, p. 77.

84 "the Arabian Nights made real": Cotton, *Yankee Bullets*, p. 23.

84–85 "a Minie ball passed through": Cotton, *Yankee Bullets*, p. 71.

85 "all bandaged and propped": Cotton, *Yankee Bullets*, p. 68.

85 "suddenly a shell came down": Cotton, *Yankee Bullets*, p. 68.

85 "succeeded in getting my": Cotton, *Yankee Bullets*, p. 68.

85–86 "frightened, rushing into": Cotton, *Yankee Bullets*, p. 68.

86–87 "Mother instantly decided to leave": Cotton, *Yankee Bullets*, p. 69.

87 "Father was horrified when": Cotton, *Yankee Bullets*, p. 69.

87 "My father's powerful voice": Cotton, *Yankee Bullets*, p. 24.

87 "here, under the shadow": Cotton, *Yankee Bullets*, p. 23.

87 "Don't cry, my darling": Cotton, *Yankee Bullets*, p. 27.

88 "In this cave we sleep": Hoehling, *Vicksburg: 47 Days*, p. 127.

88 "bear themselves like": Hoehling, *Vicksburg: 47 Days*, p. 127.

88 "rang the bell, robed": Cotton, *Yankee Bullets*, p. 29.

88 "The church has been": Balfour, *Vicksburg: A City*, p. 15.

89 "We are again victorious": Balfour, *Vicksburg: A City*, p. 11.

89 "There were loud cheers": Hoehling, *Vicksburg: 47 Days*, p. 65.

89 "I can't pity the rebels": Werner, *Reluctant Witnesses*, p. 84.

89 "I suppose [the women] are determined": Balfour, *Vicksburg: A City*, p. 150.

89 "The general impression": Balfour, *Vicksburg: A City*, p. 14.

Chapter 10: Dangerous Days

90 "After passing a bad night": Balfour, *Vicksburg: A City*, p. 12.

90 "rocking the earth": Loughborough, *My Cave Life*, p. 90.

91 "How very sad this life": Loughborough, *My Cave Life*, p. 81.

91 "the shot fell thick and fast": Cotton, *Yankee Bullets*, p. 69.

92 "when the shell exploded": Cotton, *Yankee Bullets*, p. 29.

92 "The victim . . . stood holding": Cotton, *Yankee Bullets*, p. 31.

92 "so near the top of my head": Cotton, *Yankee Bullets*, p. 27.

92 "Get in the cave!": Cotton, *Yankee Bullets*, p. 69.

93 "So up came the tent": Cotton, *Yankee Bullets*, p. 70.

Chapter 11: Growing Desperation

95 "When shall I expect you?": Schultz, *The Most Glorious Fourth*, p. 111.

95 "I am waiting most anxiously": Schultz, *The Most Glorious Fourth*, p. 111.

96 "The wound I had received": Frederick Grant, "With Grant at Vicksburg," p. 6.

96–97 "I saw a great deal of": Frederick Grant, "With Grant at Vicksburg," p. 6.

97 "Almost every day as I drove": Wheeler, *The Siege of Vicksburg*, pp. 186–87.

97–98 "He said casually, 'I guess'": Flood, *Grant and Sherman*, pp. 179–80.

98 "I then asked about her husband": Kennett, *Sherman: A Soldier's Life*, p. 355.

101 "From the remarks of some": Wheeler, *The Siege of Vicksburg*, p. 177.

102 "They agreed with us perfectly": Werner, *Reluctant Witnesses*, p. 84.

Chapter 12: Empty Stomachs

104 "all lived in a state of": Cotton, *Yankee Bullets*, p. 28.

104 "one lady standing": Cotton, *Yankee Bullets*, p. 71.

104 "Sometimes a cave had twenty": Korn, *War on the Mississippi*, p. 140.

105 "as she was about to do so": Cotton, *Yankee Bullets*, p. 29.

106 "Give them a chance": Graham, *The Blue and the Gray*, p. 114.

106 "If slaves seem good soldiers": Graham, *The Blue and the Gray*, p. 118.

106 "The bravery of the blacks": Arnold, *Grant Wins the War*, p. 284.

108 "Our provisions were becoming": Cotton, *Yankee Bullets*, p. 70.

108 "a half-barrel of [corn] meal": Cotton, *Yankee Bullets*, p. 31.

109 "It was awful, either rubbery": Korn, *War on the Mississippi*, p. 150.

109 "and pea meal": Arnold, *Grant Wins the War*, p. 272.

109 "I have rarely heard a murmur": Hankinson, *Vicksburg 1863*, p. 70.

109 "Graves are dug today": Winschel, *Vicksburg: Fall*, p. 103.

Chapter 13: Surrender!

111 "If you can't feed us": Schultz, *The Most Glorious Fourth*, p. 172.

112 "This is my only hope": Schultz, *The Most Glorious Fourth*, p. 264.

112 "I know we can get better": Schultz, *The Most Glorious Fourth*, p. 265.

113 "Dysentery had pulled me down": Frederick Grant, "An Interview With," p. 3.

114 "Soon a white flag appeared": Frederick Grant, "With Grant at Vicksburg," p. 7.

114 "Pemberton and I had served": Schultz, *The Most Glorious Fourth*, p. 341.

115 "Father was immediately joined": Frederick Grant, "With Grant at Vicksburg," p. 7.

115–16 "I remained in the tent": Frederick Grant, "With Grant at Vicksburg," p. 7.

116 "All was quiet": Cotton, *Yankee Bullets*, p. 71.

116 "We were all sitting outside": Cotton, *Yankee Bullets*, p. 71.

117 "pale as death and with": Hoehling, *Vicksburg: 47 Days*, p. 275.

117 "Such a scene of desolation": Schultz, *The Most Glorious Fourth*, p. 367.

117 "A huge plantation wagon": Hoehling, *Vicksburg: 47 Days*, p. 288.

118–19 "How sad was the spectacle": Schultz, *The Most Glorious Fourth*, p. 360.

119 "men felt very bitterly": Cotton, *Yankee Bullets*, p. 71.

120 "You can imagine our feelings": Werner, *Reluctant Witnesses*, p. 90.

120 "Our men had had full": U. S. Grant, *Personal Memoirs of U. S. Grant*, p. 295.

Chapter 14: The Unfinished War

123 "Johnston evidently took in": Korn, *War on the Mississippi*, p. 142.

123 "Really, it was very": Julia Grant, *The Personal Memoirs*, p. 128.

124 "I stopped and looked back": Arnold, *Grant Wins the War*, p. 298.

124 "Vicksburg, with her": Loughborough, *My Cave Life*, p. 145.

125 "a popular conquering general": Hoehling, *Vicksburg: 47 Days*, p. 287.

125–26 "I should think soldiers": Schultz, *The Most Glorious Fourth*, p. 390.

126 "Hunger and misery": Twain, *Cave Life During the Siege*, p. 5.

127 "had some trouble in": Julia Grant, *The Personal Memoirs*, p. 135.

127 "was the last man who": Cotton, *Yankee Bullets*, p. 67.

128 "admired courageous persistence": Cotton, *Yankee Bullets*, p. 34.

128 "As we stepped aboard": Cotton, *Yankee Bullets*, p. 34.

129 "I never want to live": Cotton, *Yankee Bullets*, p. 19.

Afterword

132 "My son accompanied me": U. S. Grant, *Personal Memoirs of U. S. Grant*, p. 255.

132 "I could not leave my post": Kennett, *Sherman: A Soldier's Life*, p. 209.

ACKNOWLEDGMENTS

My first conversation about the story I hoped to tell in this book was with Vicksburg's own Gordon Cotton, the now-retired director/curator of the Old Courthouse Museum. Gordon introduced me to the reminiscences of children who became part of my story, and welcomed me to Vicksburg when I came to see it for myself. He also shared with me his extensive knowledge about life during the siege, and I am indebted to him. I am also grateful to his then-assistant, Jeff Giambrone, for his help. The current staff at the museum, especially George "Bubba" Bolm, director/curator, have provided valuable assistance with information and photographs. Terrence Winschel, historian at the Vicksburg National Military Park, helped clarify several factual inconsistencies. Betty England, now retired, gave me a memorable tour of the battleground. The staff at the British Library in London assisted me with source material. Meg Chorlian, Hilda Hands, Greg Schultz, and Linda Meyers also helped me. I am ever indebted to my agent Regina Ryan, and to my editor Melanie Kroupa and others at Farrar, Straus and Giroux. As always, I am sustained by my fellow scribes Barbara Bartocci and Deborah Shouse, whose advice is endlessly helpful and whose friendship is my rock.

ILLUSTRATION CREDITS

Every effort has been made to trace copyright holders, and we apologize for any unintentional omissions. We would be pleased to insert the appropriate acknowledgment in any subsequent edition of this book.

Cook Collection, Valentine Richmond History Center, 129 (left)
The Crawford Collection at the U.S. Army Military History Institute, 139
Library of Congress, 2, 12, 13, 14, 16, 20, 28, 31, 32, 33, 36, 47, 51, 52, 57, 58, 62 (left), 63, 67, 76, 82, 83, 101, 104, 105, 106, 118, 128, 136, 137, 138, 150, 158
Massachusetts Commandery Military Order of the Loyal Legion and the U.S. Army Military History Institute, 30, 79, 112, 129 (right), 145
National Archives, 18–19, 23, 48, 96, 99, 159
Adapted from National Park Service Data, 46, 50, 68
Old Court House Museum, Vicksburg, Mississippi, 6–7, 10, 39, 41 (left), 41 (right), 71, 74, 86, 100, 107, 119, 123, 125, 131, 141, 157
Picture Collection, The Branch Libraries, The New York Public Library, Astor, Lenox and Tilden Foundations, 25, 91, 114

Southern Historical Collection, Wilson Library, The University of North Carolina at Chapel Hill, 62 (right)

Image research by www.sonofthesouth.net, 53, 143

Cover Image Credits

Cover illustration and design © 2009 by Michele Bedigian, Studio 1482

Front cover: (children, from left to right) Frederick Grant, Library of Congress; Lucy McRae, Old Court House Museum; Frederick Grant, Library of Congress; Vicksburg, Old Court House Museum; battle scene, Library of Congress; newspaper articles, Old Court House Museum; family with soldiers, Library of Congress

Back cover: (top) newspaper articles, Old Court House Museum; (bottom) naval battle on Mississippi River, Library of Congress

Note: No photograph of Willie Lord is known to exist. The two boys who appear on the front cover of this book with Lucy McRae are both images of Frederick Grant.

INDEX